Dream Chasers

A Journey of Faith

ERIC SUDDOTH

Rising Smoke Publishing

Unless otherwise indicated, Scripture quotations are from:
The Holy Bible, New International Version (NIV) © 1973,1978, 1984, 2011 by Biblica, Inc. Used by permission. All rights reserved worldwide.

The Holy Bible, New King James Version (NKJV) © 1984 by Thomas Nelson, Inc. Used by permission. All rights reserved worldwide.

The Holy Bible, New Living Translation © 2004 by Tyndale House Publishers. Used by permission. All rights reserved.

The Holy Bible, The Message © 2005 by NavPress. Used by permission. All rights reserved.

The Holy Bible, English Standard Version (ESV) © 2007 by Crossway Bibles. Used by permission. All rights reserved.

The Holy Bible, International Standard Version (ISV) © 2011 by The ISV Foundation. Used by permission. All rights reserved.

The Holy Bible, The Bible in Basic English (BBE) © 1965 by Cambridge University Press Used by permission. All rights reserved.

The Holy Bible, New International Reader's Version (NIRV) © 1995, 1996, 1998, 2014 by Biblica, Inc.
Used by permission. All rights reserved.

Excerpt taken from *The Lessons of St. Francis: How to Bring Simplicity and Spirituality into Your Daily Life* by John Michael Talbot are copyright © 1998 by John Michael Talbot. Used by Permission of Plume. All rights reserved.

Rising Smoke Publishing
ISBN 978-1-949869-05-7

We all have a dream

We all have a purpose

It's time to use your dream to fulfill your purpose

Contents

Forward

Jim Rayburn, the founder of Young Life Christian ministries for teenagers, said, "It's a sin to bore a kid with the gospel." I would like to expand that to include all people regardless of their age! The full gospel of Jesus Christ is about living a new abundant life in Him and through Him. We find this abundant life through spending time with our Father daily in an abiding relationship. Often somewhere along our journey with Him we will tend to wander, question, doubt, and even wonder if God still loves us. Eric has gifted his readers by writing this book that will reawaken this dream of love that God has for us. This is not a fairytale – like book of ducks, puppies, and rainbows, but one that God can use to reveal the importance of our journey with Him. Come along and encounter the Dream Maker and Dream Revealer as you walk through the pages of *Dream Chasers*. – Mark B. Weaver, author of *I Wish I'd Paid Better Attention in Vacation Bible School*

http://wishidpaidbetterattention.com/

Preface

I need to be honest with you before you continue reading. I do not have any formal theology education. I have never been to seminary and am not a preacher. I am just a man who works at an accounting firm during the week and leads a group of high school boys at my church. Some may believe that I don't have the qualifications to write a book about faith. A degree can't give the real-life experiences that I've had. They may not be glamorous tales of journeys through exotic lands, but a person's faith doesn't exist only after walking on foreign soil. The journey of faith can happen anywhere if you are willing to take the first step.

This book does not contain new revelations. It's a collection of hard-earned insights for people from someone who knows that God is faithful. He could have asked anyone of more status to write this book. Yet I feel called to deliver a message I feel that God is telling me to share.

I have walked down the road of faith, sometimes aimlessly; running into obstacles that seemed overwhelming and immovable. Yet through it all, I found that God is walking that road beside me. I have taken my focus from Him and watched my certainty disappear. Yet I have learned that God never let me down. When we are doing something God has called us to do and given us a passion for, He will provide the way for us to fulfill the plans that He wants accomplished.

In this book, I want to be a vessel to give hope. I want you to have hope that anything is possible, because with God there is nothing that is impossible. If there is one thing in this world I want to accomplish, it is to give a little help to those walking without a purpose or believe they have no calling. I have been there, and it is not fun when you feel like you are between a rock and a hard place. I know I don't have all the answers, but the one thing I do know, without a shadow of doubt, is that God does. Keep walking in faith. You only fail when you sit down and give up.

Don't give up. God is with you.

Peace

Chapter 1

Are You Sure?

Picture yourself swabbing the deck; manning the wheel; hoisting the anchor and raising the mast as you set sail on a journey of a lifetime. Holding onto the rails of a massive ship, you wave goodbye to the familiar seacoast to ride upon tides that have been the foundation of folklore for centuries. Legends of great sea creatures that lie beneath the black abyss are spoken of with intrigue. Now you're hanging over the edge, staring at a reflection from the heaven while waves smack against the finest piece of craftsmanship of your generation.

Let's get real. You probably would rather see yourself enjoying the sea on a cruise ship with their endless buffet tables and party atmosphere. Or you may see yourself on a yacht, experiencing the life of the rich and famous as you sail along the French Riviera. So, let's set a time period for our imagination. Let's sail the uncharted seas 500 years ago as the first mate for Christopher Columbus, Ferdinand Magellan or Bartolomeu Dias to name a few. Can you feel the excitement in the air? You have been told all your life by everyone you love and trust that the world is flat. That if you sail close enough to the edge, the unthinkable will happen…Splat! Most people would cling to the solid land of familiarity or the safe life, some would say. But you, you believe there is something more. Something more than what you have been told all your life.

Can you imagine the ridicule that Columbus must have faced? "You are crazy! You can't sail west and reach India. You will fall off the earth." Some people would continue to dream silently, but when you feel certain about something, you hold on to it no matter the cost. He first went to King John II of Portugal, who said no. What a humiliating experience to enter the courts of John II only to be rejected.

Let's put this into perspective. Think of a dream that you have or an idea that you have heard that sounds crazy. It could be about digging a hole in the ocean floor to gain entrance into a new civilization under the earth's crust or building a city on the largest cloud in the sky. What about creating a fuel source that runs entirely on laughter? Now that we have what some people might see as outlandish ideas, we need investors. We go to the President of the United States. Even if I get an appointment to sit down with the leader of the free world, I can see him picking up his phone and dialing security as I mention a lost civilization. Even with the phone in his grip, would you stop if you felt passionate about this idea? Would you stop as you are being escorted out of the White House and asked never to return?

What did Columbus do? He didn't stop. He went to King Ferdinand and Queen Isabella of Spain. We all know the story of Columbus. How he set sail with Spain's blessing in the hopes of reaching India. How he found the "new world" of the Americas instead. Yes, Ferdinand and Isabella agreed to Columbus' request, but it took eight years before they agreed to supply Columbus with what he needed to begin the voyage.

Eight years of planning. Eight years of standing on the coast of Spain, tossing rocks into the ocean. Eight years of walking along the sandy beaches as the tides washed over his bare feet. Eight years of waiting for something to happen without any proof that it would succeed or even if he would live to regale people with the stories of the heroic pilgrimage.

Columbus had a huge amount of faith in something that he couldn't see. There were no global maps showing foreign lands. There were no satellites with GPS telling him to sail a few thousand miles to the west where he would hit land. There were no sailors who could guide him on this expedition with knowledge of a previous route. It was a huge risk, not only for Columbus and his crew, but for the naval powerhouse of Spain. This was the age of extreme nautical exploring, and it was just the beginning.

I don't know about you, but when Columbus Day comes sailing through in October each year, it's easy to think of it as another day to buy some new linens or anything else that is 30 percent cheaper. But consider this. He was a great explorer who took a great risk. Without him, who knows? I could be sitting in Wales eating fish and chips or getting ready for my afternoon tea.

Instead, by his determined belief in something more, one man changed the face of the known world. All because he had some faith.

Do you have that type of faith?

As a kid, I loved history class. I loved learning about the past and reading the exciting stories. As I read about Lewis and Clark and their journey to the Pacific, Neil Armstrong and his one giant leap, or Marco Polo's winding trail to China, it was as if I was the brave explorer. Isn't it always easier to be brave when you know what the outcome will be? This reminds me of a song by Chris Rice "Eighth Grade" where he recalls moments from his past that he once believed were crucial moments. He states that it's safer to look to the past than the future because you already know the outcome of your past. And he is so right. We already know the conclusion of our struggles ten years ago.

What are some things you worried about ten years ago? Looking back, were they worth the worry?

Marco Polo, who acted courageously, was most likely a little scared. When he made it to China, he probably felt safer traveling through the foreign lands of yesteryear than the mysterious tomorrow. Isn't that how life is? Having faith in the unseen is often harder than having faith in something you can see.

But if you act on something based on what you can see, is it really acting on faith?

We hear the expression from parents, siblings, and pals, "I knew you could do it. I had faith in you." It is usually said after an accomplishment, a giant hurdle that was cleared with or without the utmost ease. I can remember hearing my mother say those encouraging words after a test my junior year of college when I thought I had failed. I remember making a phone call after leaving my Intermediate Accounting class (don't let the name fool you, it wasn't intermediate). It was a lovely September day. The sun was shining, but I felt like it was the grayest day in history. I knew that I had blown my first test. I always thought I would go into accounting, but my sophomore year didn't go so well, making me doubt myself and my abilities. I knew that it would only get harder as the years progressed. There I was in my junior year and I was determined to do better. I studied like crazy for the test. As I left the class that day, my confidence had been shredded. "Mom, it was hard…really hard."

The next day I was prepared to see an F on my paper with a note from the professor telling me to quit the accounting program and move on to something that my brain was more qualified to handle. Something perhaps like basket weaving. To my surprise, the F had a few other lines turning it into a B. I was so relieved that I immediately called my mom. "I knew you could do it," she said. "I had faith in you."

I know the phrase was used to pat me on the back while pinning a "Job Well Done" button onto my shirt. Did she really have faith in me that I'd pass the exam? Or do we just use the word "faith" as carelessly as we use the word "love." I hope you *love* this book.

I hear people often use the cliché that they have faith in the chair that they are sitting. That they have faith in the airplane soaring in the sky. They have faith in electricity. It's easy to say that I believe a wooden object with four legs underneath a solid slab of oak will hold my body weight so I can sit comfortably without falling between the moving molecules that make up the mass. I may not have studied aerospace engineering, but airplanes have been in flight for more than a century now. They continue to get larger and faster and millions of people use this mode of transportation daily. So I can assume that it would work for me if I decided to fly to Boston to gallivant along the Freedom Trail. Lastly, I have no clue how electricity works. I do know that when I push the power button on my television it will broadcast an image recorded in Hollywood in 1964 with crystal clarity. I also know that when I am home in the evenings I will be sitting on my couch watching Netflix.

Is believing that the chair, the plane or electricity will work as intended really equivalent to the choice of faith?

So it comes down to this: Is faith something so common these days…or have we lost the reverence for the word faith?

Hebrews 11:1

"Now faith is being sure of what we hope for and certain of what we do not see." New International Version

"Faith is the confidence that what we hope for will actually happen; it gives us assurance about things we cannot see." New Living Translation

"The fundamental fact of existence is that this trust in God, this faith, is the firm foundation under everything that makes life worth living. It's our handle on what we can't see." The Message

"Now faith is the substance of things hoped for, the evidence of things not seen." New King James Version

I love the different translations of this one verse. Faith should not rely on what we know, see, hear, sense or experience. Faith is something that should come out of nothing, from it's creator – God. It is being confident in what we do not see. This seems like a contradiction. How can you be sure in something you cannot see? That's where so many go wrong when it comes to faith. Most want proof. God, the Maker of all that we see and cannot see, can reveal Himself anyway He wishes. He could spell His name in the stars. He could cause birds to sing His name. He could do anything, but if He did those things to reveal His glory, what would be the use of having faith in Him? Would we still see Him as God or some arrogant superpower magician?

When the mystery writer of Hebrews scribbled down these God-breathed words, I wonder if he or she realized the depth in this one sentence. The book of Hebrews is a book written for the new Jewish-Christians to show how their old faith in Judaism flows into faith in Christ, the Savior of the world. Faith in Christ was revolutionary. It was scary for this group who were taught from infancy that a messiah would come to redeem His people. Much to their surprise, and to many determined disbelief, He came. During their lifetime Christ walked the earth; performed miracles; died for the sins of humanity; was buried in a tomb for three days and rose victoriously from the dead to walk on the earth for another 40 days before ascending into Heaven. It was nothing short of a three year 40 day whirlwind. Can you say, "Um...slow down please. I'm still trying to wrap my finite mind around you feeding thousands of people a few months ago with a few fish and bread?"

Can you fathom what a radical change it must have been for the Jews to accept Christ as their messiah? Most of them, had lived their lives within certain spiritual boundaries. They had studied and memorized the Torah. They offered Yahweh sacrifices as forms of penitence or gratitude. They went to the temple. They prayed and followed strict guidelines of purification, among other Divine stipulations. Then Jesus happens. Now there is a drastic change, kind of like a huge insert, as their image of a savior takes form of a carpenter from Nazareth. The transition must have been hard. For many, very.

It's just as hard today for many to come to know Christ in a personal relationship. Preachers can tell you all that you need to do to have faith. Mentors and teachers can guide you through your journey of faith with scripture and prayer. Family can raise you in church and surround you with faith-based experiences. You can know all there is about faith in God, and yet not truly have faith in God.

"You believe that there is one God. Good! Even demons believe that – and shudder." James 2:19 New International Version

Is your faith in the One who causes the powerful ebb and flow of tides anchored to a feeling of happiness? Is your faith in the Holy Father like an inheritance that you received from your parents because they believed in Christ? Is your faith in the Creator of the universe centered like the sun in our solar system to something you saw?

I don't want to undermine anyone's faith or say that you can't be a Christian because you found God in a certain circumstance. That would defy scripture. Because in Romans 10:9 it says:

"That if you confess with your mouth, 'Jesus is Lord' and believe in your heart that God raised Him from the dead, you will be saved." New International Version

What I'm asking – and I hope you answer with complete honesty – are you sure of your faith in Christ Jesus even though you can't physically see Him in all of His glory? Are you sure that if your life ends in the next 15 seconds that you will stand before the Lord of lords? Will you bow down to Him in reverence and hear Him say those beautiful words, "Well done my good and faithful servant. Welcome home my child."

If not and you wish to solidify your faith in Christ Jesus, say this prayer with me. Don't just say the words like reading a book. Say them with a pure heart. Say them as if you caught sight of your childhood best friend across the airport and this is your tearful reunion. Say it with meaning. He loves you. He has stopped what He is doing to listen to you right now.

"Dear Jesus, I know I am not perfect. I have done some things in my past that I wish I could take back. Please forgive me. Thank you for Your love. I believe with all my heart that You died a horrible death. You died my death so that I would not have to experience a separation from You for eternity. I believe You rose from the grave and defeated death. Thank you for being the God who is forever in control. Jesus, I love you. Thank you for saving me. I will try to live my life to please You until I meet You in Heaven. Sweet, sweet Jesus. Amen."

If you said these words for the first time, Heaven is throwing a party bigger than Time Square on New Years Eve. Just stop and think for a moment that angels are screaming in excitement. God is pointing from heaven like a new and very proud dad in the hospital, "That's my kid!" You are His child. You will never be alone again. I hope you are feeling like Columbus as you start this new journey. It will not be easy. Neither was His, but you will not be going through it alone.

I hope you're sure about your salvation. I hope you are certain with unwavering faith that Jesus is the Lord of your life. I pray that you continue walking the path God ordained for you long before the angels caught a glimpse of the creation of the world. I long for your assurance so you can continue on this journey to discover the many layers of faith. Salvation is just the beginning of your faith. There is so much more. So whatever comes, even the darkest trials of life, I hope you can cling to Hebrews 11:1.

"Now faith is being sure of what we hope for and certain of what we do not see."

Aren't those some sweet words to hold onto when life is rocking?

They sure are.

Chapter 2

Hope...What Are You Hoping For?
"Now faith is being sure **of what you hope for**..."

When you read the name Edward Jenner, what comes to mind? Do you think about your first grade chum you played with on the monkey bars? Is the name similar to a distant cousin that lives in Memphis and works as an Elvis impersonator? Maybe the name doesn't have any significance at all, and you're wondering, "Why am I thinking about a name I haven't heard before?"

Let me give you a little background on Dr. Edward Jenner. Dr. Jenner was born in Berkeley, Glochestershire, England on May 18, 1749. At the ripe young age of 14 he started his training to become a doctor. He later completed his education and training in London. While a physician, he noticed something. In his hometown, the milkmaids who handled cows daily rarely contracted a disease that caused many to lose their lives. He recognized that since these milkmaids came in contact with this disease, they were immune from getting the deadly illness. In 1796, with much hope, Jenner tested his theory by exposing James Phipps, an 8-year-old boy, with blisters from the hand of a milkmaid. The wait was probably equally agonizing for the family of James and Jenner, who had purposely exposed the boy to a disease in hopes of saving his life.

With relief, James suffered with a small fever and became resistant to cowpox, which is a mild form of smallpox. This was a giant leap in the science of immunization. The theory of immunization had been tested sporadically throughout history, but never proven to work in all cases. Dr. Jenner continued his research to stop smallpox – one of the most feared diseases at the time. This disease killed up to 33 percent of those who contracted it. Dr. Jenner quit his medical practice and devoted himself totally to research and development of immunizations.

Many thought that Jenner's theory was ludicrous and had serious doubts about his findings. Dr. Jenner had hope that this new discovery was capable of something greater so he continued walking the sometimes narrow scientific road. Thanks to Dr. Jenner's determination, in 1979, the World Health Organization declared smallpox extinct.

Sometimes faith mixed with hope can be a powerful combination.

———————

When I was in middle school, I remember distinctly that I wanted to be a biochemist and work in a research lab to find cures for all the diseases that affect us today. I wanted to be the modern-day Dr. Jenner or Dr. Jonas Salk (who discovered the vaccine for polio). But in seventh grade we had a fieldtrip to a hospital. I was excited and nervous because the only time I had been to the hospital was to see my cousins after they were born. We roamed the halls that reeked of the sterilized aroma that fills every hospital. I was feeling good until we came to a room that had test tubes with thick crimson liquid all over the counters. As I felt my knees weaken and my stomach flip, I knew that my days of dreaming of discoveries were over. My hope was dashed.

I still believe that I would have been an awesome scientist. I believe as a scientist, I'd have an unrelenting dedication and excitement in finding the answers behind the finicky cells that seem so small, but can pack a devastating punch. Apparently, God had another plan for me.

God puts dreams and hopes in all people, but each dream is different. Yes, there may be some similarities. Some pieces that I hold may fit together with someone else's that can be used to help me along the way, but they are not exactly the same. God created us uniquely to tap into the perfect will that He planned for us. Just because a scientist in California is working past midnight trying to find a vaccine for cancer – which is exceedingly important – doesn't mean that the hope God placed in you is any less vital. He or she may find the vaccine that could save billions in the next century (keep the faith and hope in your searching doctor). While your hope fulfilled might only affect a handful, it's not the size of the dream that matters, but the dream itself. If God placed something on your heart that you are hoping for, keep hoping.

There is a reason that He chose you. You may be the only person who can complete it for Him.

Jesus said, "You did not choose me, but I chose you and appointed you so that you might go and bear fruit – fruit that will last – and so that whatever you ask in My name the Father will give you." John 15:16 New International Version

Isn't that a fascinating thought? God chose you to have the dream that you have now. Don't give up. Don't let go of hope. When Jesus said to go and bear fruit, He is not talking about the edible goodness. He is saying to go and do it. If there were two trees in the yard, one an apple and one a pear, could you tell one tree from the other if the tree didn't have fruit on it? I can't, and most likely you couldn't either unless you're an arborist. They would each be large with limbs and leaves. But when they start growing the fruit, we can tell what type of tree they are. They fulfilled their purpose.

We are like those trees. People can look at us and see that we are humans. They can't figure out what talents and strengths lie within because we are not living our life the way God appointed us to live. We just live like non-descript trees in a forest. But God made you different. He made you unique. He made you to not just be a regular tree among the masses. He made you to do something that no one else will do. So, go and bear fruit that will last.

What talents and strengths do you have? Are you using them?

Faith and hope are mentioned together many times throughout the Bible. There is a heavenly bond that brings these two words together. Faith is important, but if you don't use your faith, what use is it? Hope is always important, but when what you hope for falls through the first time, you might give up and your hope will be gone. You need faith to continue hoping and you need hope in order to have faith.

Hebrews 10:23

"Let us hold unswervingly to the hope we profess, for He who promised is faithful." New International Version

"Let us hold fast the confession of our hope without wavering, for He who promised is faithful." English Standard Version

"Let us continue to hold firmly to the hope that we confess without wavering, for the One who made the promise is faithful." International Standard Version

"Let us hold tightly without wavering to the hope we affirm, for God can be trusted to keep his promise." New Living Translation

I think the mystery writer of Hebrews could not have explained the correlation between hope and faith any better than in this verse. When the going gets tough, and it will, don't lose your hope. Hold tight to the faith that you have, because if God gave you something to hope for, He will provide a way for you to receive it. God is so faithful. He is more faithful than the rising sun which comes around everyday. Maybe He made the sun to remind us each morning. If a star in the heavens is that faithful, how much more faithful is its Creator?

To be clear, there is a difference between God's plan and our plan for our life. The American dream is a plan with which people grow up. Get a good education; find a nice job; get married; have 2.4 children and a dog and live in a two-story house surrounded by a white picket fence. This is the plan. Just because it's your plan, does not mean that it's God's plan for your life. It is tricky to figure out what your destiny is in God's plan. Some people struggle their entire life over following God's will. Yet they do nothing because they say they don't know what God wants them to do.

I understand it's hard sometimes to hear God. He doesn't always answer us in an audible voice. But if you listen, by stopping and taking the time to go one on one with God, He will talk to you. In fact, He would love to talk to you. Often we go to God in prayer and we do all the conversing. However, prayer is a dialogue. Do you enjoy speaking to someone who never takes a breath for you to say something? Do you enjoy hearing about your friend's weekend, when they don't even bother to ask you about yours? Do you enjoy listening to someone's problems, but they never allow you to give advice that may be helpful in resolving the issue? God wants you to speak to Him, but just like a friend, He wants to speak to you as well.

Are you listening? He is more than willing to talk.

When you pray, who speaks more? You or God?

———————

Do you remember a time when you dreamed about something? A period when you would have done anything to achieve your goal? A season when you set your sight on the stars? During this journey you probably knew, without a doubt, that it was just a matter of time until you reached your destination.

Did you? Did you finally reach the pinnacle of your reason for life? If you did, I am so happy that your hope was not fruitless.

"Hope deferred makes the heart sick, but a longing fulfilled is a tree of life." Proverbs 13:12 New International Version

Many of us are not as fortunate as some to fulfill their dreams so quickly. I want you to think about what you hoped for 10 years ago, but never received. Are you still holding onto the hope or has years eroded the once firm ground causing you to stumble and to give up?

Why do you think you didn't see your dreams fulfilled? Were your abilities not good enough? Was the timing off? Were the cards dealt to you so horrible that not even a master card shark could have made a winning hand out of them? I know in my past that when I hoped for something, and in some situations, still hope for, I tend to question myself and God.

"Are you sure you can do this Eric?"

"Are you sure God that you want me to do this?"

It always seems that when we start to ask ourselves the questions that you only ask when no one is around, doubt takes the driver's seat and boots hope to the back.

So, is asking questions wrong? Does it weaken ones faith to say, "I don't know?" Is asking the Maker of everything a simple question wrong?

I remember as a kid, my family called me motor mouth because I would not stop asking questions. I was a precocious third-grader who turned any moment of silence in the car into a grilling session of hows and whats?

I asked the typical questions about nature and science. I asked why we do what we do? Sometimes my family could answer them, and sometimes they couldn't. Just because they couldn't answer me, I didn't stop asking. I kept right on with my inquisition. As a child, my mother would read to my sisters and I Bible stories like Jonah and the whale, Daniel and the lions' den, Queen Esther, the miracles of Jesus and all the others. I believed the stories were true. I had faith in what I was reading and hearing, but I just didn't understand it all. Once again my mom would try to answer the questions, but sometimes they were beyond her own understanding. Not saying that she isn't intelligent, but there are countless questions for which no one knows the answers.

One day while in Sunday school I started to ask the teacher a question. She turned to me and said, "You just need to stop asking questions and have faith."

Is that how God responds to us?

I may not be the most intelligent man on earth, and I am not close to being the wisest, but I don't think we should ever stop asking questions. I don't think the God of the universe is uncomfortable with our questions. I don't think I can concoct a question so hard that I would stump the God who formed the language of DNA. I also don't think I can pose a query and lay it at my Savior's feet and He would just kick it away in annoyance.

A favorite Bible story of mine is found in Mark 10. The disciples are gathering around Jesus and a group of children come to Him. His disciples start shooing the children away and say that Jesus is too busy to speak to children. Jesus didn't nod in agreement. He didn't puff out His chest and say, "Your little minds are too fragile to come into my presence. Please leave."

No. Jesus said, *"Let the children come to me."* Think about a time when you have been around kids. The kids I see are pretty comfortable to say anything to anyone. "Why do you have such a big nose? Why are your legs so hairy? Do you have any kids? Do you make a lot of money? Why aren't you married?" They are not shy and they ask questions, no matter how personal or degrading they may appear. Jesus could have just talked with the children, which I believe He would have enjoyed. The incident, however, became a teaching tool. The children were His examples of real faith.

"I tell you the truth, anyone who doesn't receive the Kingdom of God like a child will never enter it." Mark 10:14b New Living Translation

Does God look at you as an example in order to show other people how to have a life of faith?

Is your faith and hope worthy of being admired, even by God?

———————

Earlier I asked you to think about hopes and dreams you had in the past that may not have been achieved. I hope you've lived a life where you had hopes and dreams. My sister tells me that I sometimes dream too much. I don't think you can ever do that. I have many dreams that I've yet to see fulfilled. That doesn't stop me. Please don't stop hoping or dreaming. Don't stop because I asked you to. Continue hoping because God planted that desire in your heart. There is a purpose for it, but once you give it up, it is so hard to get back.

Think about how you felt when you first started to date the love of your life. Some of us will have to pretend, but don't lose heart, don't give up hope. Was the time full of smiles, laughter, and butterflies in your stomach every time he or she touched your hand? Would you spend all night just staring up at the stars and listening to your loves breathing pattern while on the phone. When you are in love all you want to do is be with that person. Let's fast forward to where we are now. Three months to 70 years may have passed. Are you still filled with as much passion as you were back then? I hope you are. I hope the love of your life is still and will always be the love of your life. Sadly, life happens. Jobs become the priority, children take the focus or home renovations move front and center, and you begin to live a life as friends. The passion is gone. I hear people say in the movies, "Where did we get off track? Where did we get all messed up?"

The simple answer is they lost their passion. They didn't even realize they lost it until it was too late. I am not saying that you can't get your passion back or that God can't heal rocky marriages. Once the flames have died down, it is hard to start a fire with ash and embers. That is why so many people give up on their dreams and start new ones when they realize they have a desire for something again. Whose to say that wasn't God's plan for them to lose their drive 15 years ago, just so they could finally find their true plan in life. I'm not God, and God is so much wiser than me. So who am I to say that couldn't happen. All I'm trying to say, sometimes in a clumsy two left footed way is, it's hard to get hope back once you let it fly away. Don't let your hope go. What a sad life to live.

I don't want to lose my passion. I want to have my faith burn inside me so hot and so bright that I can't hold it in.

"But if I say, 'I will not mention His [God] word or speak anymore in His name,' His word is in my heart like a fire, a fire shut up in my bones. I am weary of holding it in; indeed, I cannot." Jeremiah 20:9 New International Version

I enjoy listening to the story telling of Sara Groves. One of my favorite songs, "Jeremiah," comes from her album, *The Other Side of Something*. She sings a song wanting to know more from Jeremiah about the fire in his bones. I have been in that spot where I felt something, but I didn't know where to go. I knew that God had planted a desire in my heart to do something but sometimes, just like Jeremiah, we fumble and say that we are just going to look past it. We go our merry way, but God's fire isn't a tame fire. No, it is powerful. It is all consuming. When God lights a fire in your heart, no water can quench it. Our stubbornness not to follow, can.

In the book *The Lessons of St. Francis*, John Michael Talbot stated, "Francis saw persecution as the smoke that accompanies the fire of a burning love for God." The first time I read this line I was taken aback. I had not ever thought about smoke being the proof of a passionate life for Christ. When we see smoke, we know there is a fire somewhere. If we follow the trail, we find from where the source of the fire is coming.

So my question goes up: Do you see the smoke in your life?

The harder question may be, can others see your smoke?

"Now faith is being sure of what we hope for and certain of what we do not see."

Do you have any hopes and dreams? I don't mean things like making an A on a test; getting a raise or buying a new dress. These things are nice but God wants us to dream big. He doesn't want us to settle for an hors d'oeuvre when He has a fillet mignon feast waiting for us.

He wants us to experience life to the fullest with all the ups and downs. He wants to walk through the valleys with us. He is always walking with us, but He wants us to walk with Him, no matter what is happening. Then when we are celebrating, He is celebrating. He is not a shadow that just follows us everywhere we go. He is so much better. He is there not just to run to when we need rescuing, but a God we can turn to and with whom to hold hands. He's a God to love and by whom we are loved. No running needed. He is always with you.

Lastly, find your hope and dreams. Once you do, cling to the hope. Don't ever let it go.

Dr. Edward Jenner was a student of Dr. John Hunter who repeated Dr. William Harvey's advice. The sixteenth century English physician said, "Don't think, try."

Don't sit on the side lines anymore. Come on and try.

"Let us hold unswervingly to the hope we profess, for He who promised is faithful." Hebrews 10:23 New International Version

When you're standing at home plate with bat in hand, get ready. Life is always ready to throw you a ball. There are many things you can do when the pitcher releases the ball. The one thing you don't want to do is waver. As the ball comes speeding toward you, take your stance. Hold tight to the bat, knowing that God, your biggest fan, is cheering you on from the bleachers. Stand strong and courageous because Christ dwells in you, and He conquered death, so you can conquer anything. If the ball is good, swing with all your might. If the ball is too high or out too far, wait for a better pitch. If the ball is about to drill you in your side, absorb the blow. Don't swerve. Don't flinch. Don't step away.

You may not ever get another opportunity. In baseball, when the pitcher hits the batter, the batter gets to walk to first base. It may not have been the way you wanted to get on base, and you may have a bruise the next day, but rejoice. You made it to first.

Not everyone makes it that far.

Chapter 3

Certainly Is Definitely a Possibility

Now faith is being sure of what you hope for and **certain**...

When you think about history, what comes to mind? Do you see yourself sitting in high school listening to a man with different colored socks, lecturing about the fall of the Roman Empire in a boring monotone voice? I wish some teachers would make the study of history more interesting. History is very interesting. Whatever time period you study, there is something exciting. You can't find a century or even a decade where nothing happened. Scandals occurred as frequently in the Dark Ages as we see them broadcasted today. Monumental events occurred often within politics, technology, arts and all the other different aspects I could categorize.

In history, we study the new forms of transportation, great works of art, the birth of new civilizations and discoveries of ancient relics. But how often do we hear about the failures? Is history only filled with experiencing new and better things? No. History is filled with broken dreams, just like today.

Harland David Sanders was born in Henryville, Indiana, on September 9, 1890. When Harland was six-years-old, his father passed away. His mother was forced to start working to support the family. Since his mother was working, he became the household cook, preparing daily meals for the family. Harland had a difficult childhood. After being abused by his stepfather he dropped out of school and ran away from home. Instead of finishing the seventh grade, he became a farm hand. At 16, he lied about his age and joined the U.S. Army. Harland had many jobs when he was young – steamboat pilot, insurance salesman, and railroad fireman, to name a few. It seemed he was never afraid to try something different.

While Harland was working for the railroad, he attended Southern University where he earned a law degree. He practiced law until he was around 40 years old. His career ended when he physically fought a client in a Little Rock, Arkansas courtroom.

Even with all of his hard work and determination, it seemed like his life was filled with defeat after defeat after defeat. Eventually, he ended up in Corbin, Kentucky, where he opened a service station. Harland noticed that many travelers who stopped for gas were usually hungry. Ding! Ding! Ding! He had another idea. He would start serving them food. He didn't have a restaurant inside the service station, so he served the customers from his living area adjacent to the service station. Word spread about Harland's cooking. Especially, his chicken. He started working as a cook in a local motel which had its own restaurant. Here he continued perfecting his secret chicken recipe. Harland's reputation continued to spread throughout state, and in 1935,

Governor Rudy Laffoon granted him the title of Kentucky Colonel.

In 1937, Harland tried starting a restaurant chain in Kentucky, but it failed. Two years later, he had the idea to open another motel and restaurant in Asheville, North Carolina. That failed as well.

During the next 20 years he worked to perfect his fried chicken recipe, which he eventually did. He once again started a restaurant in Kentucky and it became a success. But in 1956, bad luck struck again. He went broke when the government constructed a new highway that bypassed his restaurant. To make ends meet he traveled throughout the United States, trying to get restaurants to use his fried chicken recipe. It is said that he was rejected 1,009 times before a restaurant accepted it. Yes, I said 1,009 times! But he was certain of the product that he had.

Harland David Sanders is commonly known to millions of fried chicken lovers around the world as Colonel Sanders. The founder of Kentucky Fried Chicken or KFC summed up his journey with this, "I made a resolve then that I was going to amount to something if I could. And no hours, nor amount of labor, nor amount of money would deter me from giving the best that there was in me. And I have done that ever since, and I win by it. I know."

Colonel Sanders not only had faith in his abilities, but also hope for the future and determination that he'd make it. Maybe the ups and downs of the journey taught him to value life and not money. Instead of hoarding his earnings, he turned over his profits to churches, hospitals, the Boy Scouts, and the Salvation Army. He also adopted 78 orphans from other countries. I love one of his quotes, "There's no reason to be the richest man in the cemetery. You can't do any business from there."

Are you certain that you can achieve your dreams?

If the answer is no, then why not?

———

Why do we have such a hard time believing in ourselves? We say we have faith in the almighty God. We say that we know God can do all things, and we hope that we see Him do just that.

We say, we say, we say. But do our actions prove that what we say is what we believe?

It's so easy to say that I have faith in God, because those are just words. Sometimes I think we use that phrase as a cop out because we are putting all the balls in God's court, and if it doesn't work out we just say, "Well, it wasn't in God's plan."

Truthfully, we do hope for things that sometimes aren't in God's plan. There are other times that we don't even try. To be clear, God doesn't need our help to do things. He can do anything. He just sometimes wants to use us to spearhead His miracles.

There is the old proverb where a dam breaks and water floods an entire city. A man climbs to the top of his house and sits and prays to God to save him. He watches as the waters rise over his gutters. Two men in a boat come by, "Hey, do you need any help? We have room if you want in our boat?"

The man on the roof replies, "No, I am okay."

The men in the boat leave confused, but what could they do?

The man on the roof again prays to God. Suddenly, another boat comes by with a man and a woman who themselves were apparently saved from the flood waters. The water is now over part of the roof, creeping closer to where the man sits. The man shouts as he tries to get close to the roof, "Hey, come get in our boat."

"No thank you! I'll be okay," the man on the roof shouts back, shooing the man and woman away.

The water continues to rise and is just a few inches from his feet. He screams out to God, "Please help me!" Another boat comes by, this time operated by an elderly gentleman. "I've come to help you," he said. "I almost missed you, but I just heard you scream. Why are you still here? Did the other boats not stop for you?"

"Yes, but I am okay. You go on," the man on the roof said.

"What? You need to get in the boat now," said the elderly man.

"No, you go on. I will be okay."

"Are you crazy? Please young man, just get in my boat," the older man pleads.

"No. I will be okay."

The elderly gentleman leaves in his boat heading to safe ground.

The water continues to rise until it covers the entire roof, causing the man on the roof to slip and fall into the water. He floats down the rushing river and drowns.

When the man on the roof got to heaven, he is furious. "I need to talk to God," he rants to an angel.

"Yes, I believe He wants to speak with you as well," the angel answered as they walk along the golden streets. They are quiet until they reach God who is sitting on His throne.

"I am so mad at you! Why did you let me die? Did you not hear my prayers? How could you ignore my pleas when I was dying?" The young man screams in God's face without any sense of respect.

"My poor child, I heard your prayers. I would never have ignored you. I didn't want you to die," He said in a soothing voice. "I sent three different boats to save you."

The man crumbled at God's feet.

Isn't that how we are? We put all our faith in God to do it all, when we won't even get in the boat.

Are you still waiting for an answer to your prayer when God may be giving that answer it in a different way?

————————

Are you asking God for an answer, but already have the only one you'll accept in mind? If you have done this, or are doing this, don't feel bad. I know I have been there. Even the disciples did the same thing.

The disciples loved Jesus. He was their teacher, their leader, their brother, their friend. Jesus was everything good in human form. The disciples believed that Jesus was the conquering Messiah. They had total faith that he would defeat Rome and restore Israel to its former glory. They read the scriptures that prophesied His coming. They heard His teachings that cut to the hearts of those who really listened. They saw the miraculous signs that only the Messiah could perform. Yet, when Jesus told them the plan God had for His life, they didn't believe it.

They had a vision of the Jews rising up and getting their freedom back. They desired a general who would stand up for their rights and regain control. They yearned for a king with a backbone to suppress the people who had oppressed them for many years. They imagined something other than Jesus being crucified on a criminal's cross. Their plan for their Messiah was different than God's for the Messiah.

So, if you have prayed with an answer in mind, don't feel like a failure. Just know that you are in good company. Look at the great things the disciples did in Jesus' name after His death and resurrection. You may have prayed a selfish prayer in the past, but the past is behind you. The future is full of possibilities and blessings. Dive into them.

Let's look at someone who prayed for something, struggled with God's answer, but ultimately, surrendered to His plan:

"Jesus went away a second time and prayed, 'My Father, if it is not possible for this cup to be taken away unless I drink it, may Your will be done.'" Matthew 26:42 New International Version

Jesus prayed this prayer a little while before He was arrested, beaten, and crucified for our sins. Jesus had the power to stop the guards from arresting Him. He had the power to escape from the shackles. He had the power to call the angels out of Heaven to rescue Him. Yet He didn't. He was not looking at His mortal will, but God's will for His life. When you pray, be ready to follow.

Be ready to surrender.

———————

When you talk to God, how do you interpret what is happening? Do you see Him as an available ear or do you believe that the God of the universe is listening and will answer your prayer? Because the Bible assures us that He always answers ours prayers – either yes, no or wait.

I love Psalm 5:3. Love it!

"In the morning, O LORD, You hear my voice; in the morning I lay my requests before You and wait in expectation." New International Version

I love to read Psalms! These poems and songs cover every emotion, every situation, every high and every low that we face. David, a writer of many of the Psalms, was a man after God's own heart. But David did some things, I am proud to say, that I have not. If God can love David through all of his scandals, God certainly can love me. And He most certainly loves you as well.

When we pray, it should not be as a last resort with us, not caring what happens. No. When we pray, we should go to God in reverence and honor that He is taking the time to listen to us. Then with excitement, we should watch and wait with certainty that He will answer.

What do you want to ask God for right now? Let me clarify, God is not a genie that grants every wish. But He is a God that gives blessings when they are asked in agreement to His will. If you have faith in God, and you have hope in the request, now you need to ask with complete certainty He will answer. He is waiting for you to ask.

Go ahead, ask.

———

Hopefully, you have gone before and asked Him for something without any reservations or strings attached. By strings I mean saying, "God, if you do this one thing, I will do whatever you want." God does not barter with us. As believers, we should surrender to doing whatever God wants us to do every day.

Therefore, make your request with a pure heart. God wants you to hope and dream, but He will only fulfill those in the way He has planned. Cling to the promise in the previous chapter.

"Let us hold unswerving to the hope we profess for He who promised is faithful."

When we ask, remember that,

"With God, all things are possible." Matthew 19:26 New International Version

---

So, are you certain that anything is possible?

"For I am certain that not death, or life, or angels, or rulers, or things present, or things to come, or powers, or things on high, or things under the earth, or anything which is made, will be able to come between us and the love of God which is in Christ Jesus our Lord." Romans 8:38-39 Bible in Basic English

When you are one in Christ, nothing can come between you and God. Trials will come and try to get you off track, but don't lose hope. Stay close to God. When an incident arises and your faith starts to crumble, remind yourself that nothing can separate you from God. This is a verse that I say to myself all the time when I feel distant from God to remind myself that God is here. Life happens, but God is still here.

God is still God.

God is still good.

I went to a conference a few years ago, and I heard Beth Moore speak. It was an awesome experience. She taught about how God equips us (Hebrews 13:21). She said God uses every incident in our lives to make us who we will become. There are many things in life I am grateful that I did not experience – loveless home, a tragic death, childhood abuse. But Beth Moore said God can use all those incidents for His glory.

You may become angry while reading those words. You may have wounds that have not healed. I've not walked in your shoes, and I admit that my life has probably not been bad compared with others. But I just want to remind you that God loves you. He didn't want you to go through what you went through, but He allowed those tragedies because He could see the good that could come out of it.

The story of Joseph drives this point home. Joseph was sold into slavery by his brothers, but eventually became one of the most powerful men in Egypt. After being reunited with his brothers, Joseph said,

"You intended to harm me, but God intended it for good to accomplish what is now being done, the saving of many lives." Genesis 50:20 New International Version

With an outlook like Joseph, what could get you down? Yes, he did have horrible times: betrayed by his brothers, sold into slavery, falsely accused, imprisoned, and forgotten by comrades, but did he ever lose hope? No. As a young man, God gave him visions, so he knew that something better was coming. He probably had days where he felt rejected by God, but he didn't become a slave to those emotions. No, he knew that God would prevail. He was certain that what man had intended for bad, God would turn into good.

Do you believe that?

You may think that nothing good could come out of those dark valleys, but read what God said to Paul in the book of Philippians. The book is filled with so much joy that you would think that Paul was on a beach somewhere watching the sunset without a care in the world. It couldn't be further from the truth. When Paul wrote his book of joy, he was in prison or under house arrest. Paul lived a life that no one would wish to live, yet he lived it with joy. Listen to what God told Paul to write,

"And I am certain that God, who began the good work within you, will continue His work until it is finally finished on the day when Christ Jesus returns." Philippians 1:6 New Living Translation

Yes, it may be painful, but it is good. When it is finished it will look good, because God is good. Who knows what God has in store for your future, because of your past? Could you use your history to help others? Anything is possible.

May you always remember you are loved. God loved you so much that He sent His son to die a horrible death, so you would not have to.

How great is the love the Father has lavished on us that we should be called the children of God. – 1 John 3:1 New International Version

You are one of God's children. He wants nothing but the best for you. You are loved by the God who created love. How awesome is that!

Do you believe you are loved to death?

You are.

———

Thomas Edison tried more than a thousand times before he invented a working light bulb. He was certain that he could do it, and he did. The American inventor, who knew struggle, defeat and victory said,

"Many of life's failures are men who did not realize how close they were to success when they gave up."

"Nearly every man who develops an idea works at it up to the point where it looks impossible, and then gets discouraged. That's not the place to become discouraged."

"I have not failed. I've just found 10,000 ways that won't work."

Now faith is being sure of what we hope for and certain of what we do not see.

Are you certain?

Chapter 4

Blind Faith

Now faith is being sure of what we hope for and certain **of what we do not see**.

Can I get an amen from all the runners out there! I love to run (or I used to before my knee injury). I may not be the fastest or the best, but I just love to run in the late evenings when the stars are shining down on me. It's a great time to let the stress of the day fall away. It's also a good time to reflect on the day, or if you run in the mornings – which I don't wake up early enough do to – a good time to seize the day.

Many people may not get an adrenaline rush from running. But if I don't run for a few days, I feel like I'm missing out. When I travel to a different city and see people running, I feel envious as they are sweating up a storm, and I sit pigging out on my double cheeseburger. Well, we all got to eat.

When I run, I usually have a set path. I sometimes run up and down my street or downtown, or even when I feel really athletic a track at a nearby school. I rarely run without any notion of where I'm going. My distance changes by how much time I have, but more often, it depends on how long I can last before my legs feel like jelly. When I run, I look around at the scenery, or I fix my eyes on something ahead to motivate me to make it to the end.

A few Octobers ago, I finished my first half marathon. Yes, I was only man enough to do a half marathon, but who knows what the future holds. Every year I watch snippets of marathons they televise and am in awe of the runners' speed, tenacity, strength, and dedication.

One runner which invokes much respect in the running world is Marla Runyan. Marla is a marathon runner. She is a three-time national champion in the women's 5,000 meters. She is a two-time Olympian who finished eighth in the 1,500 meters in the 2000 Sydney Olympics. In the 2002 New York City Marathon, she finished as the top American. Oh, did I mention she is legally blind?

Yes, this woman who can run circles around the average human without breaking a sweat is blind. She could let her vision impairment run her life, but she doesn't. She just runs. She was the first legally blind athlete to compete in the Olympic games.

On a few occasions, I've closed my eyes as I ran in order to relax. I can only make it a few steps before I pop open my eyes to watch the ground. Talk about blind faith. Marla demonstrates it superbly. Next time you go for a run or a walk, try it with your eyes closed. Feel the uneasiness in your movements. Feel the fear of the unknown. Are you nervous about cracks in the pavement that can trip you? Do you wonder if you will bump into another person, causing them pain or even making yourself look foolish?

When I watch Marla run, she is focused. She is driven. She is running her race to win it. Even though she can not physically see the finish line, she knows there is one and she runs for it.

We all may not run a marathon, but living a life of faith is a similar experience. We all have a finish line. The difference in our races, is the reason for the race, and the prize waiting at the end.

———————

You know what else I love about running, how it is mentioned quite a few times in the Bible.

"Therefore, since we are surrounded by such a great cloud of witnesses, let us throw off everything that hinders and the sin that so easily entangles, and let us run with perseverance the race marked out for us." Hebrews 12:1 New International Version

Running is not something you can take up one day and participate in a marathon the next. You need to keep at it. You need perseverance. In life, we need to keep at it, even when it gets hard. We need to run with perseverance the race, the dream, the plan, or the goal, that God marked out for us.

When I ran in a half marathon, I had this idea that I would be able to do it flawlessly. I mean, the most I had run before was five miles, and I was going to jump to thirteen. I knew my body would be tested, but I thought I could overcome it because I had a finish line to run toward.

The first five miles went smoothly, like they always do. Then I embarked on foreign territory. My legs started telling my body, this is new. My muscles began protesting. "We have never been here before." But I kept running. There were many times that I thought I would just fall over, but I had a mission, so I kept moving. At mile eight, my legs were shaky. I knew I needed to slow down. I stopped running.

I felt horrible. I was not going to be able to run a full marathon, but I didn't stop. I started to walk. When my body started to feel refreshed after a few minutes, I knew it was time. I started to run again. It would have been easy to stop and watch the rest of the runners pass me by. But I was surrounded by a cloud of other witnesses – fellow runners. I knew that if they could do it…I could do it. I didn't finish my marathon in the time that I wanted. Surprisingly, I was just a little behind the time in which I wanted to complete it. But when I finished, I didn't care about times. I had persevered. I had finished.

I love that the verse says that I am surrounded by a cloud of witnesses. I can imagine in my daily walk that the saints and angels are with me. I may not see them, but if I look close enough I can see their footprints. Billions of people have been on this earth before us, and they had the same type of struggles that we have. But they got through it. This gives me so much hope. If they can walk a life of faith, then I can. There's a song that I sing every once in a while when I'm alone with my guitar.

I can see the footprints
of the saints who have gone before
and if I close my eyes,
I can see them by my side
along with the Lord
Help me Lord, to keep this pace,
keep the faith,
oh, keep this pace,
to finish this race.

When I run, I don't carry weights or backpacks, or anything that can hold me down. All I have are the clothes on my back. If life is like a marathon, why do we carry so much baggage? The Bible says to throw off everything that hinders and the sin that so easily entangles. Do we just love to suffer?

Sometimes the baggage we carry, we carry for good intentions. It's great to be involved in church; go to Bible studies, teach Sunday school classes, sing in the choir, cook dinners for the pastors. But sometimes we do so much good, that we miss God.

I remember a story of a woman whose family life was a mess, but she was at church every time the doors were open. She taught church classes, played the piano for worship, and sang on Sunday mornings. All the while her home life was crumbling. Years after her divorce, she was talking to me and she said, "I had good intentions. But my marriage may have been fixed if I stopped doing the 'church thing' and worked on my marriage with my husband." This was a hard lesson that she learned a few years too late.

I know there have been times in my life where I tried to please men instead of trying to please God. I taught the classes, I hosted Bible studies, I showed up at the volunteer events because I was single, and I had time to waste. I mean, what else could I do? If I didn't show up, people would ask me where I was. Then one day, I realized that even though I felt like I was doing God's work, I wasn't.

God wants to use us, but I was using God to gain a good reputation.

When God calls us to do something, He says that He will give us the strength to fulfill it. But so often, we try to do everything ourselves without God's strength. We proudly crawl on the ground, dragging a weight that God could carry with ease.

Throw off all that hinders you, and run the race with God. Just keep the pace.

———

"Then they came to Jericho. As Jesus and His disciples, together with a large crowd, were leaving the city, a blind

46

man, Bartimaeus (that is, the Son of Timaeus) was sitting by the roadside begging. When he heard that it was Jesus of Nazareth, he began to shout, 'Jesus, Son of David, have mercy on me!' Many rebuked him and told him to be quiet, but he shouted all the more, 'Son of David, have mercy on me!' Jesus stopped and said, 'Call him.' So they called to the blind man, 'Cheer up! On your feet! He's calling you.' Throwing his cloak aside, he jumped to his feet and came to Jesus. 'What do you want me to do for you?' Jesus asked him. The man said, 'Rabbi, I want to see.' 'Go,' said Jesus, 'Your faith has healed you.' Immediately he received his sight and followed Jesus along the road. Mark 10:46-52 New International Version.

Every time I read one of the miraculous healings that Jesus performed, I am amazed. I am amazed that God of Heaven was in flesh and with a single word healed the blind, lame, possessed, even the dead. On the other side of the coin, I am amazed at the faith these people had in Jesus.

I can see the blind man sitting along the side of the road with other beggars, listening to stories about a man named Jesus from Nazareth. I can see someone telling a farfetched tale about a man in the next town over who was crippled from birth, but when Jesus touched him, he was able to jump to his feet. Can you see the group laughing at the man telling the story? "No one can do that. Don't get your hopes up. This Jesus cannot do that. He is from Nazareth."

Suddenly, the group of beggars heard a crowd nearing them. Not just any crowd, but a large crowd surrounding one man, Jesus. Do you think their hearts stopped? Do you think they felt the power of God which was now a few feet from them? Or do you think they just passed this man off as a fraud?

We don't know how many beggars were healed. We only know that in this instance one was recorded in the Bible. One would think that when they noticed that their friend had been healed, that they would all be screaming at Jesus for help. There was probably chaos, but only the blind man is mentioned. Why?

Was the blind man alone on the road? It is a possibility since he is the only man mentioned, but usually back then beggars sat together in groups. The blind, the mute, and cripples were frowned upon because society thought a sin had caused the disability. No one wants to suffer alone, so they would usually congregate.

My theory, and it's only a theory, is that it took a lot of faith for the blind man to ask to be healed. Then when the others asked, it wasn't in faith. They were only asking because they just saw Jesus heal their blind friend. At that point, they didn't need faith.

So, I just pose this question, which one are you?

The man with faith, or the one who has witnessed a miracle just a second too late?

———————

True faith is when you believe in what you cannot see. When you take a step without knowing where you're going to plant your feet. Is your faith strong enough to ask blindly?

"This is the confidence we have in approaching God: that if we ask anything according to His will, He hears us. And if we know that He hears us – whatever we ask – we know that we have what we have asked of Him." 1 John 5:14-15 New International Version

We need to approach God with confidence. We don't need to approach God as if He is a genie in a bottle, and we have three wishes. No, God is not a genie. He is worthy of honor. He is worthy of all our praise. He is without a doubt, unquestionably, worthy. The reason we can approach God with confidence is not because of the confidence that we have in ourselves, but the confidence that we have in God to be able to do anything. Nothing is too difficult for Him to accomplish. There is no task that will cause Him to sweat. There is nothing that would make Him stutter in fear of messing something up. God is perfect! That is the confidence that I have. I'm not perfect, but my God is!

So I will kneel before the almighty God with holy reverence and ask Him for help. It isn't a self-centered plea, because when my motives are pure before God, I shouldn't be ashamed to ask

Him anything. When I humble myself before my King, I will not want to ask self-seeking prayers to better myself. I will only ask for things to bring Him glory.

When we ask anything according to His will, He hears us! I don't think a period does that statement justice. We need to be bold in our confidence in Him, and Him alone. Oh, He hears us when we are broken before Him. He hears us when we don't know where to turn. He hears us! He hears us! HE HEARS US!

Can I get an amen?

——————

One of my favorite singer-songwriters is Ginny Owens. On her first album, *Without Condition*, she started out singing the classic hymn, "Be Thou My Vision." It was a good accapella rendition; her soothing voice was fragile yet strong. As I played through the rest of her album, I was drawn to the honesty in her words. I felt everything that she was singing. I felt the pain, but I felt the hope that Christ is strong and God is good. One of my favorite songs on the album is, "If You Want Me To." If you have never heard this song before, please listen to it.

This song just gave me the faith to know that yes, life is hard. It isn't going to be easy, and God never promised life would be smooth sailing. I cling to a line in her song, where she is holding onto the promises God has and her assurance that He's not finished with her yet.

Oh, those are such good words to hear when you are down in the valley. God is not finished with you. God is still working on you. He still has big plans for you even when you don't see it.

After I wore out my compact disc, I was talking to a friend about the album, and how I loved every song. She agreed. Suddenly, she started talking about the first song on the album, "Be Thou My Vision." I said I enjoyed it too, but she just stared at me.

"Enjoyed it? She is living that song," she said.

I listened as she talked, and I didn't understand what she meant. How did she know that Ginny Owens was living that song? I thought my friend had just become engrossed with Ms. Owens, on the verge of being a stalker, to know that her life is that song.

I think she realized that I was missing the point. She said, "Eric, you know she's blind don't you?"

I felt so dumb, but it all made perfect sense. "Be thou my vision oh Lord of my heart..." I wish we all had this prayer for God to be our vision. Sometimes we miss out because we see so much.

A few years later I heard Ginny Owens singing my favorite song of her's at a concert. This time she added another stanza about anticipating her celebration when she's going to cross over her proverbial Jordan and get to Heaven. She sang that she's going to look God in His eyes and see that He was always there beside her through all the valleys and fires she walked through. The song gets me every time I hear it.

Isn't that an awesome viewpoint in life?

May you take a step of blind faith and experience life with all the good and the bad. And when you, cross over your Jordan, I hope you are going to rejoice and look into His eyes and see He never let you down.

Chapter 5

Sing, Sing, Sing
A Life of Worship

Do you love to worship? I mean, do you get excited about the chance of throwing yourself into a place where you can lose control for one purpose? Many people would probably say that they worship, but do they love it? They may have to say no. Then why is it that at sporting events, people wear their team uniforms proudly or even paint their faces with those loyal colors? Why do they scream and cheer when their team scores, and then cry and yell when the opposing team does the same? Is this not worship? Some people work 60 hours a week to get a nice paycheck, and then buy a prize for their hard work...is that boat, nice car, new outfit not something that they worshipped? Some may get defensive and say they don't worship these things. But worship doesn't just constitute singing a song in the honor of something. Worship is giving something undivided attention. Worship is longing for something. Worship is what we sometimes do best without knowing that it is worship.

I wonder if James Naismith, the inventor of basketball, knew what type of worship his sport would inspire. I wonder, if he was alive today, how he would he feel to see so much devotion to the sport that he birthed. I also wonder his feelings because in 1890 he received a degree in religion from Presbyterian Theological Seminary in Montreal and volunteered for the Kansas National Guard as a chaplain in 1916.

I am not saying that sports are evil, because I love athletics. But when we say to ourselves that we don't like to worship, that basically means we don't like to live…and living is good.

So, what do you worship?

In my daily walk with Christ, I don't know where I would be if I did not worship daily. I do not have the luxury of having a worship service to attend each day, but worship is not bound by a church setting. Worship can be anywhere.

I try every morning, some mornings not too well, to wake up with a heart of thankfulness and joy. I love the Chris Tomlin song "Awakening" that I try to sing each morning.

Some mornings it is easier to sing when I feel well rested and refreshed. But I shouldn't praise my God only when it feels good. I should give praise every morning to the One who granted me another day with breath in my lungs. I should give praise every morning to the Giver of my sight for the chance to see the rising sun. I should continually give thanks to the God who loves me and will always love me.

After I leave my house, I usually enter the sanctuary of my car. I hear a lot of people say that this is their place of prayer. This may be the best chance to have a quiet moment with God in such a chaotic world. They roll up the windows, turn off the stereo, and just drive in communication with their Father. There are many days that I plead my case behind my steering wheel. God doesn't care where we talk to Him. He just wants us to talk and listen. Hopefully, listening is the key purpose in your prayers.

When my car isn't a place of prayer, it is usually a place of singing and praise. I feel so comfortable in my car that I am singing at the top of my lungs, tapping my steering wheel to the beat, banging my hands on the ceiling just to lift up His name. I am in His presence and only His.

"But I will sing of Your strength, in the morning I will sing of Your love; for You are my fortress, my refuge in times of trouble. O my Strength, I sing praise to You; You, O God, are my fortress, my loving God." Psalm 59:16-17 New International Version

———————

Worship is not just about singing, and music. I've had many nights of worship just by reading the scriptures – scriptures that are God breathed. I allow them to fill my heart. I love to read the letters that Paul wrote, and even though he wrote them for a particular church at the time, they seem relevant today. As I read them, I can picture Paul in prison somewhere, praising the God of

Heaven and Earth, giving thanks for everything. Not just the good, but also the bad things. Because it's through those God's glory has been or will be revealed.

Paul lived a life of passion before and after his conversion to following Christ. Before his belief in Christ, he was passionate about stopping the Christ revolution by any means, even murder. He was a witness to the stoning of Stephen, the first martyr for Christ (Acts 7:58). After his transformation from a Christian killer to a Christ follower, his passion was for converting non-believers to Christ. He wanted to show the love of Christ to all.

In Paul's first letter to Timothy he writes:

"This is a trustworthy saying, and everyone should accept it: 'Christ Jesus came into the world to save sinners' – and I am the worst of them all. But God had mercy on me so that Christ Jesus could use me as a prime example of His great patience with even the worst sinners. Then others will realize that they, too, can believe in Him and receive eternal life. All honor and glory to God forever and ever! He is the eternal King, the unseen One who never dies, He alone is God. Amen." 1 Timothy 1:15-17 New Living Translation

Can you see his passion? Can you see the fire in his words? Yes, we all have lived lives we wish we could take back. But those past scandals only show God's love even more. We can look back in our lives and see all the wrong we have committed. Yet God has mercy on us. He knows what we did yesterday. He knows what we did in the tenth grade. Yet despite all the muck we get ourselves into, He loves us. Our lives are walking testimonies that if God can forgive me, He can forgive anyone. In Paul's humble confession, he ends in a heart of pure worship.

"All honor and glory to God forever and ever! He is the eternal King, the unseen One who never dies. He alone is God."

How can you say these words without getting excited? All the honor and glory to God!

Reading the scriptures is worship. God told men throughout history to write down His words so we can read them today. God wanted it on paper, so we can read of His love and mercy. When John was writing, probably the most familiar verse, God wanted him to write it so you could read it.

"For God so loved the world that He sent His one and only Son, that whosoever believes in Him shall not perish but have eternal life." John 3:16 New International Version

What an awesome thought.

"I reach out for Your commands, which I love, that I may meditate on your decrees." Psalm 119:48 New International Version

Do you praise God when you read His word? It is not just another book. It is a book that God wrote through a large group of people. It is God's holy word. We need to gain some respect for this honorable and lovely book. It is a book of love. Yet it is a book of power, God's holy power. I hope you see the Holy Bible as a bound copy of love letters. Love letters to you. He was dying for you to read them.

———————

There are many different ways for you to worship and one way is not better than another. I know people who worship God while painting, some crochet, others just bask in the views of creation from a mountain top or a tree stand in the early mornings. We are all different. Just as God has a different purpose for our lives, He has different ways of worship. What I enjoy, may not be what you enjoy. You may hate to sing, so just stand in honor of your God. Find what you enjoy, and let God become a part of it.

A great worship experience, which may sound odd, is to have a date with God. Find something that you enjoy and then take God along with you. Let it be only the two of you on your night. You may love to golf. This weekend, golf alone and take the time to listen to God. You may love to cook. The next time you do, turn off the television and experience the concoction you are making from the One who grew the ingredients. I could go on and on with all the different activities you could do. The main thing is to leave room for God in your joys. He gave you that joy for a reason. It wasn't an accident. He longs to be a part of it.

There is no wrong way to worship…it's only wrong if you don't.

———————

The main point of this chapter was for you to learn to worship God with a pure heart. He doesn't want you to come to church and sing songs that don't mean anything to you. He doesn't want your leftover prayers at the end of the day when you are too tired to stay awake for three minutes. God wants all of you, and that is what worship is. All of you.

The prophet Isaiah said:

"The Lord says:

'These people come near to Me with their mouth and honor Me with their lips, but their hearts are far from Me. Their worship of Me is made up only of rules taught by men.'"
Isaiah 29:13 New International Version

We need to get right with God in our worship and get real with Him. He can see through the façade of Christian life. Your neighbor may believe you are the best person in the world, but God sees the truth. You cannot outsmart Him with your life of plastic smiles and makeup. Our worship needs to be sincere. It needs to be pure. It needs to be real. We need to be humble before the Almighty. When we are falling apart, we just need to crumble before Him and know that He is compassionate. He is loving. He is good, and He is daddy.

———————

While you are on your journey, cling to worship. If your dream has come true, you need to praise God for all that He has accomplished. You need to praise God for working through you. You need to praise God for what He has done and is doing.

If you have not reached your goal, your dream, your hope, you need to praise God for what He is going to accomplish. You need to praise God for His faithfulness. You need to praise God for His perfect planning. You need to praise God for what He is doing and is about to do.

I pray that you worship wholeheartedly. I pray that you will grow to love to worship. I pray from the bottom of my heart that we will never get tired of giving our God praise.

Hold onto the faith that God has amazing things planned and you are part of them. If you thought your plans were great, God has something better.

"As the heavens are higher than the earth, so are My ways higher than yours and My thoughts than your thoughts." Isaiah 56:9 New International Version

"So is My word that goes out from My mouth: It will not return to Me empty, but will accomplish what I desire and achieve the purpose for which I sent it. You will go out in joy and be led forth in peace; the mountains and hills will burst into song before you, and all the trees of the field will clap their hands. Instead of the thornbush will grow the pine tree, and instead of briars the myrtle will grow. This will be for the Lord's renown, for an everlasting sign, which will not be destroyed." Isaiah 55:11–13 New International Version

God has some big things planned for you, and what He sends forth will not be brought back to Him empty. Feel the power of God around you. Feel the peace as you go out into the world to accomplish the mission that He set in your heart.

Go in joy.

Go in hope.

Go forth in worship.

Chapter 6

This is Just a Test

Some say that to become a member of the elite United States Navy SEALs is probably one of the most grueling tests one would face. To become a Navy SEAL the average recruit spends more than one year in training. They have to have the physical strength to accomplish any mission handed to them. In their training, they have to swim, run, and do other strength building exercises. If they don't do the minimum amount of push-ups or swim 500 yards in around nine minutes, they will probably be let go. The Navy SEAL classes lose around 70 percent to 80 percent of the recruits. Simply put, only around 20 percent pass the test.

Not only do the recruits have to have unbelievable physical strength, they need mental stamina, as well. The Navy SEAL tackles most missions in teams. They don't want to put their lives in the hands of a man who crumbles in danger or under stress. No, their mental stability needs to be as big or larger than their biceps.

While earning my accounting degree, I had to take a Business Law class taught by a former JAG. The stories he told in class were fascinating, sometimes it seemed larger than life to know that the professor teaching us the basics of law, actually put them into practice around the world.

One day, my professor walked into class, sat down on his desk and started telling stories of when he was in a combat zone in southeast Asia. He had to walk the halls of a military hospital and write the wills of men on the verge of death. He tried to keep the graphic details to a minimum, while telling the accounts of two different soldiers.

One soldier had been shot in the head and was barely alive. The doctors gave him little hope of surviving. Another soldier was lying on a gurney with shrapnel cuts, very minor compared to the head wound. He was telling us that the soldier with the shrapnel was crying like he was dying. His wounds were painful, but he could have survived. Yet he had given up. The man with the gunshot wound to his head was hanging on for dear life. The professor looked up at the class and said, and I'm paraphrasing, "The man with cuts on his arm thought he was dying. And in a matter of days, he was dead. The man who wanted to live, even though most people thought he would die, recovered. The message behind these stories is, don't give up. I saw a lot while I was a JAG. I don't understand it, but your mind is a powerful thing. Once you give up, there is no use. You are as good as dead."

Don't be as good as dead.

———

There are many layers to a life of faith. One layer is always dreaded by me more than any other. That layer is the one of tests. In my years of education, I was a decent test taker when I knew what to study. But with tests like the ACT, SAT, CPA, and others that cover a mass of information, I never scored as well as I thought I could have. I hate true and false questions. I can read the question and it would appear true. Then I would start to dissect the question and one word would make it appear false. I hated them!

The same could be said about multiple choice questions. I usually mark out two of the answers for being wrong. The remaining two would sound alike except for one word. That one word would either cause me to get the question right or wrong. Usually, I chose wrong.

I hate to say this, but life is like a test. We have many choices. Some say that we make more than a thousand choices each day, whether it be what color socks to wear or whether to proceed with an experimental operation. Some choices are harder than others, but it is still a choice. We may not even see these as questions, but they are. Each is a question on your daily test. When you lie down to sleep, did you pass or fail today?

Many days I feel like today didn't even have a pass or fail, because nothing significant happened. If we have a day that didn't amount to anything, was the day even worth it?

Do you think God had an easy day planned for you where nothing seemed important?

"For I know the plans I have for you,' declares the Lord, 'plans to prosper you and not to harm you, to give you hope and a future.'" Jeremiah 29:11 New International Version

Looking at the life of Jeremiah, this is one of the most comforting verses. Jeremiah was a prophet during a time when God's people had turned away from Him. Jeremiah was commanded by God to stand up and repeat everything God told him to say. Most of the time, these were not easy words for Jeremiah. Is it easy to tell your government that God is mad at them? Would it be a sweat-free day to walk up to your friends and tell them all the bad things they are doing? Would it be a happy day to tell your family that God is not pleased with their actions? No, he was rejected by them all.

Jeremiah had to deal with pain and hurt daily. His friends and family mocked him. He was imprisoned; he felt suicidal; he questioned God about why he was even born. He was almost totally alone…except that God never left him. God told Jeremiah that verse to reassure him that God had plans, not just something mediocre, but plans to give him hope and a future. God has the same type of plans for you. Even though you're going through the mud right now, lift up your chin and take heart.

God has a future for you.

Do you believe it?

If you are feeling beaten right now, just consider it pure joy.

What? Did I just say to be happy when you are going through something terrible? No. I didn't say to be happy. But I said to be joyful. There is a difference between happiness and joy. Happiness is an emotion derived from something external. You are happy when you are with friends and family; you are happy when you watch your favorite television show. You are happy when you go on vacation. Happiness comes from something or someone.

Joy on the other hand is internal. You cannot cause yourself to be joyful by doing something or being with someone. Joy comes from God the Father.

When people are depressed they don't have joy. They can do things that will cause them to smile and laugh, but when they leave, they don't have that feeling of joy. I'm not saying that depressed people can solve their problems by getting joy or getting right with God. With God all things are possible, but God also uses man to perform His miracles. Who is to say that a pill which can help a chemical problem is not a miracle ordained by God. Once again, I know that depression and anxiety are real problems. These conditions even affected strong believers throughout the Bible. I just want to give you hope. Your struggles, your pain, your daily questioning, is not for nothing. You are not alone. I hope these words sink in…There are other people just like you going through similar situations. You may feel like you are alone, but you aren't.

One of my favorite verses has a very deep meaning for me.

"Consider it pure joy, my brothers, whenever you face trials of many kinds, because you know that the testing of your faith develops perseverance. Perseverance must finish its work so that you may be mature and complete, not lacking anything." James 1:2-4 New International Version

That is a hard pill to swallow…consider trials pure joy.

I was in college when these verses came alive for me. I was struggling in accounting courses, and no matter how hard I studied or tried, I just couldn't get the grades I wanted on the tests. After I studied, I would sometimes go for a jog, and I would recite the first sentence over and over to myself. One day, it just hit me.

"Yes, this is a trial. But Eric, you have to get through this trial so you can move on and do something better. This is just a stepping stone. Find joy in that this is going to lead to bigger and better things. Because if you can't complete this, you definitely can't complete whatever else God has in store."

After snapping into joyful reality, I would write James 1:2-3 on the top of all of my tests. I wrote that to remind myself that while I was suffering through a test it was going to lead me to something better. I had to persevere here, to get to where I was supposed to go. Since my name wasn't James, I bet some of my professors were confused, but they never mentioned my scribbling.

I can look back and see that God helped me through the trials in my past, but it doesn't stop there. God gives me the memory of my hard times to remind me that God helped me back then, so who am I to believe that God won't help me now or in the future? It's a cycle. If I am struggling, I can cling to knowledge that this episode is going to make my faith stronger for when I need to climb another mountain that I once thought was impossible.

I guess it is similar to P90X philosophy of the plateau effect. P90X is a fitness video where you work your body to the limits. Right when you think you can't take it any longer, you don't give up, you keep trying. Eventually, you train your body to do the videos flawlessly, but it doesn't stop there. You then teach your body new exercises to become more fit so your body never reaches a plateau. Our faith should never plateau. We should never become so strong in our faith, that we reach the day when God says, "You know Eric, you are pretty strong in your faith. I think you can just stop here and enjoy the rest of your life."

If you think you have reached the plateau of your faith...watch out.

You haven't.

"Do you not know that in a race all the runners run, but only one gets the prize? Run in such a way as to get the prize. Everyone who competes in the games goes into strict training. They do it to get a crown that will not last; but we do it to get a crown that will last forever. Therefore, I do not run like a man running aimlessly, I do not fight like a man beating the air. No, I beat my body and make it my slave so that after I have preached to others, I myself will not be disqualified for the prize." 1 Corinthians 9:24-27 New International Version

Have you gone into strict training for your faith? Have you toned your spiritual body, muscles rippling, a solid six pack? Do you run a race of faith to get a prize, or do you run just to finish?

Anyone can walk over the finish line, but it is only the strong that will run past it.

Are you walking or running in your faith?

———————

The refinement of gold is a beautiful process, similar to what happens in our lives. Miners dig into a hard rock until they find something that appears to be gold. They send it up along with other rocks to test it. After the rocks have been inspected and found to be gold, it is taken to be melted down. They put all the gold into the melting pot and wait for it to liquefy. When the gold has melted, all the particles trapped in the rock that is not gold, rises to the top. They then clean the top, as if cleaning the slate. They again melt the gold to see if any impurities rise to the top. They repeat the process until no fragments rise to the top. Once it has been refined into pure gold, it's able to be casted into rings, necklaces, bars, or anything else of value. It is a lengthy process.

The same is true for our lives. We jump into our walk with Christ, but we have to get rid of the impurities in our lives. We continue on our journey. Little trials come, and they reveal our true character. Does your impatience creep into view? Is a temper about to flare? Are you willing to backstab in order to achieve your dream? Are these qualities that God would want us to have?

No. He wants us to have the qualities that Christ exemplified. When trials come and some of our true colors shine, it may be a time of refinement. Allow yourself to show your colors. Once they are revealed, it is time to clean the slate. This trial may have occurred in order for you to see your true self and not one that you idealize in a mirror. It is so easy to live a good life when life is good. It gets hard when times get rough.

So continue walking in faith. Take the trials head on. There may be a foothold that you are unable to see, and God is trying to reveal it to you. Open your eyes of faith, and look at yourself from a different view. Try to look at yourself without any history of what you wanted to look like. You may even ask a good friend. If they are truly a good friend, they will lovingly point out your shortcomings.

A chapter I find refreshing when I'm being refined is the first chapter of 1 Peter.

"Praise be to the God and Father of our Lord Jesus Christ! In His great mercy He has given us new birth into a living hope through the resurrection of Jesus Christ from the dead, and into an inheritance that can never perish, spoil or fade – kept in heaven for you, who through faith are shielded by God's power until the coming of the salvation that is ready to be revealed in the last time. In this you greatly rejoice, though now for a little while you may have had to suffer grief in all kinds of trials. These have come so that your faith – of greater worth than gold, which perishes even though refined by fire – may be proved genuine and may result in praise, glory and honor when Jesus Christ is revealed. Though you have not seen Him, you love Him; and even though you do not see Him now, you believe in Him and are filled with an inexpressible and glorious joy, for you are receiving the goal of your faith, the salvation of your souls." 1 Peter 1:3-9 New International Version

I pray that you experience these trials with the viewpoint of grace and mercy. God is allowing you to go through these ordeals to refine you and bring you into a purer intimacy with Him. It is not done out of anger or hatred, but out of love. He wants nothing but the best for you. But to get there, you might have to endure a little pain.

When you train your muscles you have to make them move. The next day you may not be able to move at all. But in a few days, you will feel better than new and able to do more. Keep moving those muscles that God has given you – muscles of love, joy, peace, patience, kindness, goodness, faithfulness, gentleness and self-control. Keep strengthening them and never stop. Once you stop, your faith will be flabby like your grandmother's arm. Keep moving forward.

Are you as fit as you want to be?

———————

When trials come, I sometimes see it as a sign of God's faith in me. He commands that I can do all things through Christ who gives me strength. So when something big happens, God is just letting me know…Eric, you can handle this.

You too can handle it.

Chapter 7

Hello God, Are You Listening?

Have you ever felt ignored? Maybe it was from an older sibling, a love interest, or a supervisor at work. You would do anything to get their attention and just take notice of you. I have been a wallflower. I feel your pain. I sometimes enjoy being overlooked, but in the rare instances that I crave to be acknowledged, yet am ignored, it is a little disheartening.

I wish my faith was strong enough to say that I haven't uttered the words, "God, are you listening to me?" I wish my faith was firm enough that I never doubted for a second that maybe God heard my prayer that I've prayed for years. I sometimes wonder in the big scheme of things, which option is better, (1) God has been too busy to listen and answer my prayers or (2) He has answered them, but not the way I wanted Him to. Neither option brings a flutter to my heart. Does either option make your heart dance?

In faith, I know that God always hears and answers my prayers. I have always been taught that God answers every prayer one of three ways, yes, no, or wait. Sadly, it is the last two that are always the hardest to hear.

There is a story in the Bible which brings mixed emotions for me. It's the one that tells of Hannah in 1 Samuel. Hannah was married to Elkanah who was also married to Peninnah. Back then men had multiple wives, but that is not the purpose of this story. Hannah could not conceive a child, but Peninnah could. In Hannah's time if a woman was barren, the woman was considered a failure, and it was a great embarrassment to her and her husband. It didn't help matters that Peninnah would ridicule Hannah about her "failure" until she would breakdown and cry and quit eating. Have you ever been like Hannah? Felt like a failure? I know I have.

Hannah turned to the One person she could, and she prayed. She prayed wholeheartedly without reservations.

"O Lord, Almighty, if You will only look upon Your servant's misery and remember me, and not forget Your servant but give her a son, then I will give him to the Lord for all the days of his life, and no razor will ever be used on his head." 1 Samuel 1:11 New International Version

She prayed with so much devotion that Eli, the priest, thought she was drunk. After she confided in Eli about her grief and pain, he said, "Go in peace, and may the God of Israel grant you what you have asked of Him."

With great relief, Hannah conceived and gave birth to Samuel. But in keeping her vow, she gave the boy to Eli so he could do the Lord's work.

This part fills me with so many emotions. I'm happy that Hannah gave birth to a son, excited that God answered her prayer, and sorrow that she had to give up Samuel to fulfill her oath. I also feel envy. I'm envious of her faith. The one thing that she desired and prayed for, was the one thing she had to give up. Yet God, with His great love and mercy, then allowed Hannah to give birth to more sons and daughters.

We should never underestimate God's plan.

We should never underestimate God.

One of my favorite books is Psalms, because the book is so honest. The writers of Psalms do not hold anything back. They come to God with their pain, their hurt, their confusion, their doubts, their love, their excitement, their struggles, and their victories. They come to God with every aspect of their lives, and that is how we should be. We should come to God and thank Him for listening to our prayers, and continually ask Him to listen to our pleas. Here are just a few excerpts from Psalms:

"Praise be to the Lord, for He has heard my cry for mercy. The Lord is my strength and my shield; my heart trusts in Him, and I am helped." Psalm 28:6-7a New International Version

"Save me, O God, by Your name; vindicate me by Your might. Hear my prayer, O God, listen to the words of my mouth." Psalm 54:1-2 New International Version

"Listen to my prayer, O God, do not ignore my plea; hear me and answer me. My thoughts trouble me and I am distraught." Psalm 55:1-2 New International Version

"Hear my cry, O God; listen to my prayer. From the ends of the earth I call to You, I call as my heart grows faint; lead me to the rock that is higher than I." Psalm 61:1-2 New International Version

"O Lord, I call to You; come quickly to me. Hear my voice when I call to You." Psalm 141:1 New International Version

"O Lord, I say to You, 'You are my God.' Hear, O Lord, my cry for mercy." Psalm 140:6 New International Version

"Out of the depths I cry to You, O Lord; O Lord, hear my voice. Let Your ears be attentive to my cry for mercy." Psalm 130:1-2 New International Version

"Hear my prayer, O Lord; let my cry for help come to You. Do not hide Your face from me when I am in distress. Turn Your ear to me; when I call, answer me quickly." Psalm 102:1-2 New International Version

When we come to God, we don't have to be formal. We just need to come. That is all He is asking of us. Come before the King and lay down your burdens. Come before the Lord and release all your anxiety. Come before the Majesty and let go of everything that is holding you down. Most of all, just come before Him. He is and will always listen.

———————

I love Christian music, can you tell? I love singer/songwriters who write from their hearts. I don't like to hear pop candy-coated music where everything is super. Because everything is not always super. It takes a strong person to unveil themselves and lay it open for anyone to hear. I take comfort in Nichole Nordeman's songs. There are songs that hit me so hard, I almost fall to the ground in disbelief wondering, "Were you watching me when you wrote your song?" Music lowers defenses and allows everyone to stand on similar ground. One song that gets me is "Small Enough" from *This Mystery*. We often put God on a distant throne in Heaven, full of power and majesty, and forget that He is our daddy who lays beside us when we have a bad dream. When I feel like the world is in chaos, I can run to the God who gave Jupiter its rings and is also clutching my hand.

Go to God, He will always hear you.

Is there something you are hiding from Him? Let go and let God listen to you.

———————

Dear Journal...do any of you keep journals? Not one that details the events of your day, but a prayer journal? Prayer journals are an awesome way to see God move. Can you tell me what you prayed on July 23, 2008? Let me make it easier. How about Spring 2018? Did you have some important prayers during that time? I mean, it was an entire season. Hopefully, you laid your heart before the God who cares for you at least once. This one is much simpler to determine – did you have a major prayer session last night?

Well, has He answered your prayers yet?

Why do we ask God to answer our prayers and then not keep track of them? We ask them once, twice, maybe daily for a long time, but what if God answered them?

Have you said thank you yet?

———————

I have been keeping somewhat of a journal since high school. I write my thoughts, verses that speak to me, prayers that were on my heart, and anything else that comes to my heart. There are some days that I don't pick up my journal. It's on those days that I feel like I am missing something. It may just be one sentence, or even a short line that I heard throughout the day. It could be something God spoke directly to me. I know my brain is not that sharp sometimes, so I usually try to write things down. Because many times when God speaks, it will still relate to me next week, next year or even the next decade.

Every once in a while I pick up my old journals and read. It's strange how reading the old journals takes me back in time. I can see myself on my bed, in my college parking lot, or in my backyard where my thoughts were written. You would think that in the last 20 years I would not remember where I was when some of my strange little insights were written. But the weird thing is...I do.

What is even more awesome, is reading the prayers that I scribbled down. I read peoples' names that I've lost touched with, names of friends in crises, names of family members with health concerns, names of the past. It's an awesome sight to see that I prayed for my friend who needed a job, and now he is happily employed. Or another friend who was battling a sickness and to see him now, three years later, healthy...God answers prayers. But would I recount all the many miracles He performed if I did not first write them down.

I am not saying that journaling is for everyone, but just give it a try and watch God move through the pages. After you have been doing it for a little while, scan through the pages and see what God revealed to you.

There have been times that I wrote something down, not realizing the impact it would have on me later. I sometimes would write down a verse or a line to encourage a friend, only months later to find that I need encouragement myself. Guess which verse usually helped the most – the one that I wrote down for someone else. God fits everything together perfectly. Sometimes we just need to step back and wait for the chaos to slow down. Then we can see the beautiful picture that He has been painting for years. God's timing is impeccable. God's timing is perfect. God's timing is always right.

So, the next time you question if God is listening, I hope you can find some comfort that you aren't alone. We all question it from one time to another, but I hope you find greater comfort from the One who is always listening.

Keep praying...

Chapter 8

Who Are You Doubting?
Is It Really Yourself?

More than a decade ago, I was sitting at home on my lunch break, flipping through channels. For some reason, I stopped on one on which an interview was underway. I can't remember who was being interviewed or which network I was watching, but I will never forget the conversation.

The interviewee was a former beauty queen, and she was speaking about self doubt. I still don't know why I watched it because that's not something that would generally interest me. I mean, *The Andy Griffith Show* was probably on another channel somewhere.

I laid the remote down and listened to this beauty queen speak from her heart, and what she said has changed the way I see myself and the obstacles I face from that day forward. "When we doubt ourselves, what we are really saying is, 'God, I don't think You are God enough to handle this.' Because if God says, 'I can do all things through Him,' then I can do all things. But when I start to doubt if I can really do something, I'm not really doubting myself, but doubting God because He has already said all things are possible."

I sat dumbfounded. When I doubt that I can to reach my goals, I'm actually telling God to His face, "Um, I know You raised the dead; I know You led the Israelites through the Red Sea; I know You hold the stars in place each night, but I don't believe You can get me through this."

Let's just say that was a day I will never forget. That moment of change came because I stopped and listened to the interview of a beauty contestant.

It's strange how God speaks so loudly sometimes.

———————

Have you ever thought that when you doubt yourself, you are also doubting the Creator of the universe? It's a humbling thought. We pray and confess that Christ is Lord. We sing our songs and lift up His holy name. We go on mission trips to spread the glory of His message. Yet even though we say we trust Him, we unknowingly doubt Him.

How does that realization make you feel? Do you feel like you let Him down? Do you feel like your walk with Him is more like a baby crawling? Do you feel like a complete failure?

We can wallow in the pit we often dig for ourselves, or we can climb out of the grave and let God resurrect our faith. He raises the dead to live again, and our faith can as well. Get out of the pit...get up and walk with Him, even on stormy waters.

"Immediately, Jesus made the disciples get into the boat and go on ahead of Him to the other side, while He dismissed the crowd. After He had dismissed them, He went up on a mountainside by Himself to pray. When evening came, He was there alone, but the boat was already a considerable distance from land, buffeted by the waves because the wind was against it. During the fourth watch of the night Jesus went out to them, walking on the lake. When the disciples saw Him walking on the lake, they were terrified, 'It's a ghost,' they said, and cried out in fear. But Jesus immediately said to them: 'Take courage! It is I. Don't be afraid.' 'Lord, if it's You,' Peter replied, 'tell me to come to You on the water.' 'Come,' He said. Then Peter got down out of the boat, walked on the water and came toward Jesus. But when he saw the wind, he was afraid and, beginning to sink, cried out, 'Lord, save me!' Immediately, Jesus reached out His hand and caught him: 'You of little faith,' He said, 'Why did you doubt?'" Matthew 14:22-31 New International Version

"You of little faith, why did you doubt?" Those must have been some sour words for Peter to hear. It would be bad hearing God say, "You of little faith," when everyone wants to hear, "Well done."

But who did Peter doubt? Himself or Jesus?

He could not have doubted himself, because he wasn't the one causing himself to walk on water. For him to doubt himself, he would have to have trusted himself. When he walked on water, he was trusting Jesus and Jesus alone. When he took that first step, if he'd trusted Jesus some and himself some, he would have never succeeded. We can't trust God with only half of our faith. We have to trust Him with all of our faith.

When Peter began to sink, he didn't start to doubt himself. He started to doubt the One who allowed him to take the first step onto the water.

When was the last time you started to sink?

Who were you doubting?

———

How can we live in faith, yet doubt? Is our faith really true, or do we just say we have faith to deceive and console ourselves? If you find yourself wondering if your faith is real, just be honest with yourself. I don't want this chapter to be the one where you doubt your salvation. But if your faith is only used as a mode of convenience or to guarantee yourself a "golden ticket" to heaven, you are missing out on so much that God can do for you. God wants to walk the roads you walk. You don't have to walk alone. He wants to be there with you through everything. If you realize that you are using God as a crutch, well, congratulations. That is your first step to living a life of faith. Take the step of faith into total dependence on God.

Why do we have such a negative connotation for the word surrender? When I think of surrender I picture battles with soldiers waving a white flag to save themselves from death. When we surrender to Christ, are we not trying to save ourselves from death? Where the difference may lie is that when the soldiers surrender they sometimes are held captive as prisoners of war. But when we surrender to Christ, we are set free. So through surrender we receive freedom. We have the freedom to know that God is always for us and not against. We have the freedom to come face to face with God, to sit down with Him and live a life as His child. We have the freedom to live a life with endless possibilities. Who would have thought surrender is a good thing?

When we surrender ourselves to God, we are giving our lives for a larger cause. It is a cause that can't be defeated.

"Jesus looked at them and said, 'With man this is impossible, but with God all things are possible.'" Matthew 19:26 New International Version

With God, everything imaginable and unimaginable is possible. I am not saying that everything we desire we will do. But if it's in God's will, it will be done. Nothing is too hard for our God. If you try to carry the load all by yourself, you may make it. If you place it in God's mighty hands, just think how lighter your load will be?

So why do you want to go through all the "heavy lifting" when God is ready, willing and able to lift it for you?

"If God is for us, who can be against us?" Romans 8:31b New International Version

When I read this verse, I sometimes take the question mark out and put an exclamation. You can read this verse like a question, but I would rather read it as an anthem. If God is for me, who can stop me! Do you feel the verse inside you? Do you feel the victory here? Do you feel the power that God is with you every step of the way? So why doubt? Why fumble in your faith? Why take a step back in fear at the first sign of trouble when God is for you?

This reminds me of when I was a kid and all the boys talked about their dads. "My dad is stronger than your dad."

"No way, my dad is way stronger than yours."

"Get out of town, my dad can lift over 100 pounds."

"Well, my dad can lift over 200 pounds."

And so on and so on.

Have you had this same debate with your fears?

"Well, my Dad is bigger than you."

"No Eric, your Dad cannot handle me."

"Yes, my Dad can handle you." If God is for us, who can be against us(!) No question needed.

———————

"But you belong to God, my dear children. You have already won a victory over those people, because the Spirit who lives in you is greater than the spirit who lives in the world." 1 John 4:4 New Living Translation

Do you understand that when you receive Jesus Christ as your Lord and Savior, He is with you? The second you made the proclamation to God, He gave you the best gift anyone could give – the Holy Spirit. The Holy Spirit is powerful, but often overlooked. Jesus said to His followers that He must leave so the Holy Spirit could come, and they would do greater things than Jesus.

The same Holy Spirit that came upon the disciples is still the same Holy Spirit today. Jesus told His disciples that they would do greater things than He (John 14:12). That means, that we should do greater things than Jesus did.

Do you believe that?

The power to raise the dead is in you. The power to calm the seas is in you. The power to heal the blind is in you.

Do you believe it?

Believe it.

This is a hard verse for me to read, but one that sticks with me every time I face a situation.

"If you falter in times of trouble, how small is your strength!" Proverbs 24:10 New International Version

I don't want to fall or stumble every time some obstacle is in my way. I want to succeed. I want to prove that my faith is real and stand the test. I don't want the world to see me as a man who says one thing about faith and then crumble when something happens. Help us God not to falter. Help us to prove to the world that our faith in You is strong.

On Sara Groves album, *The Other Side of Something*, she has a disc with an interview where she explained her songs. I was listening, because she is one of my favorite artists, and I love hearing how people develop their ideas. As I was listening, I felt God enter the conversation. She mentioned a time – not long after her first son was born – that she was touring.

"What I wanted in this last season of my life is I wanted a guarantee from the Lord that my kids and I would always be safe. I wanted to read somewhere in the Word that nothing bad will happen to you as long as you serve the Lord. I think safety is a big theme, especially, with Americans right now. We are all wanting safety, and there are so many scary things going on, and the President is constantly promising us that he can make us safe. And the Lord has been talking to me about this, because I want to know that we are safe. At my lowest point in my doubting and questioning God, I was with a friend on the bus and I said, 'If something was to happen to Kirby while I was out doing what I believe is God's call on my life, I don't know if my faith would survive that.' And she had the wisdom to look at me and say, 'If your faith won't survive that, your faith isn't surviving. If the Lord isn't the Lord of that situation, of that circumstance, if you can create a scenario where He isn't God, then He isn't God right now.'"

After I heard this I was amazed at the insight of Sara Groves' friend. "If your faith won't survive that, your faith isn't surviving."

If what you're most afraid of occurred, would your faith survive?

This is a hard question to answer truthfully. If it's an easy answer, you may need to reflect a little more.

———————

One of the best examples of doubting oneself, and ultimately, doubting God, is the story of Gideon (Judges 6-8). I would recommend reading these few chapters to see what a frightened man Gideon was, yet God pursued him. Just like God still pursues us.

The story of Gideon begins with the Israelites afraid and under oppression by the Midianites. The Israelites prayed to God for help, and God sent an angel to one man, a very scared Gideon.

"The angel of the Lord appeared to Gideon. He said, 'Mighty warrior, the Lord is with you.'

'But sir,' Gideon replied, 'you say the Lord is with us. Then why has all of this happened to us? Where are all of the wonderful things He has done? Our parents told us about them. They said, 'Didn't the Lord bring us up out of Egypt?' But now the Lord has deserted us. He has handed us over to Midian.'

The Lord turned to Gideon. He said to him, 'You are strong. Go and save Israel from the power of Midian. I am sending you.'

'But Lord,' Gideon asked, 'how can I possibly save Israel? My family group is the weakest in the tribe of Manasseh. And I'm the least important member of my family.'

The Lord answered, 'I will be with you. So you will strike down the men of Midian all at one time.'

Gideon replied, 'If You are pleased with me, give me a special sign. Then I'll know that it's really You talking to me. Please don't go away until I come back. I'll bring my offering and set it down in front of You.'

The Lord said, 'I will wait until you return.'" Judges 6:12-18 New International Reader's Version

Gideon not only gets an angel to come to him, but he also gets God speaking to him as well. And he still doubts. He keeps making excuses about their past and how his tribe is the weakest. He reminds God that he is the weakest in his family. He even leaves God and asks the Maker of everything to wait. Do you feel like Gideon? Do you make excuses when God commands you to move? Do you quickly think of 25 reasons not to follow God? Has He ever steered you wrong before? So why would He start now?

Well, to finish the story, Gideon asks God for a sign. He doesn't ask for just one sign, or two, but three signs. I guess the first one did not suffice for poor ol' Gideon. Yet God gave Gideon the signs he needed.

When Gideon was going to battle, God told him, "You have too many men for Me to deliver Midian into their hands. In order that Israel may not boast against Me that their own strength has saved them, announce now to the people, 'Anyone who trembles with fear may turn back and leave Mount Gilead.'" So 22,000 men left, while 10,000 men remained.

This must have made Gideon uneasy. He was probably wondering, "God, what are you doing? We need all the men we can get to fight." But God had another plan.

"But the Lord said to Gideon, 'There are still too many men.'"

I can see Gideon's lip fall to the ground. Too many men, "Um, God, um, are you sure?"

When God was finished, Gideon's army was down to 300 men, when it was originally 32,000 soldiers. Gideon trusted God, because I guess he finally realized that God was the One who would win the battle, not the soldiers. That is exactly what happened. Gideon's men blew trumpets and caused so much confusion in the enemy camp that the Midianites started to turn on each other.

Would your faith have survived this?

We need to realize that it is all God. He just uses us as somewhat like a partner. If we follow what He commands, take all the pressure off of us and give it to Him, where can we go wrong?

―――――――

"He must become greater; I must become less." John 3:30. New International Version

When we realize that God is in control and that we are not, a shift occurs on our faith scales, and it's a good one. But if you believe you hold all the weight and measure, then He needs to become greater and you need to become less.

A simple concept on paper, but hard in application.

If you realize that all your dreams are possible, but have doubted in the past, good news – it's a new day. The old is gone. The past is behind you. The last mile you walked is a distant memory. Keep going, but now believing that it is God who is going to finish it. He is just going to let you experience the miracle.

On the other side of the coin are you not achieving your dreams because you think they are too far-fetched? If so, you need to become less. If you think your dreams are impossible, and you are stumped by the complexities, then why did God lay it on your heart in the first place?

Give it all to God…He can handle it.

I pray that this chapter has compelled you to reexamine your faith.

A song that I've fallen in love with recently is "Do It Again" by Elevation Worship. No matter what we go through; no matter where God calls us to go; no matter the opposing forces and negative comments, God is faithful. I would rather face ridicule and failure in the eyes of man, than deny the calling on my heart from my Savior. So, when you feel like impossible is the word of the day, or your obstacles are enormous, or you feel like you're alone, remember, you are not and they are not. You may have doubt creeping in, but you have to kill those thoughts the moment they enter your brain. You are a warrior. You have the power of Christ inside you. You are capable of doing more than you think you are – not because of your own power, skill and abilities, but because of His. You may feel defeated, but God never is. He's done it before, and He will do it again.

Chapter 9

In the Desert
Now Is the Time to Worship

An interesting chapter in the life of David's faith was the period after his affair with Bathsheba. We have to remember that David was a man after God's own heart, but his character crumbled when he saw Bathsheba. Bathsheba was a very beautiful woman, especially for King David to take notice. Because let's be honest, he could have had any woman that he wanted since he was king. One problem with Bathsheba was that she was married to Uriah, a soldier in David's army.

One night, David couldn't sleep and started walking around the roof of his palace. This was probably his place to wind down, and relax. But this evening, he spotted an interesting sight. He saw the beautiful Bathsheba bathing. Instantly, David sent some messengers to go get Bathsheba (Wrong move #1), and King David fell to temptation and slept with her (Wrong move #2).

Because of David's sin, Bathsheba became pregnant. Since her husband was away at war, it had to be David's child. David devised a plan to hide their secret. David requested to see Uriah immediately. Trying not to look suspicious, David asked typical questions concerning the war and soldiers. When David was finished with this charade, he told Uriah to go home. Because what would most men do after they have been away from their wife for so long? David thought that his plan to cover up the situation had worked. (Wrong move #3).

David got word that Uriah did not go home, but slept at the entrance to the palace. David was confused, "Why didn't you go home?"

Uriah said to David, "The ark and Israel and Judah are staying in tents, and my master Joab and my lord's men are camped in the open fields. How could I go to my house to eat and drink and lie with my wife? As surely as you live, I will not do such a thing."

Uriah had noble character, because he could not truly enjoy himself when all of his men were still in the battle zone.

David has one more move – to let Uriah die in battle. "Put Uriah in the front line where the fighting is fiercest. Then withdraw from him so he will be struck down and die." Uriah was murdered (Wrong move #4). David may have deceived himself that he didn't murder Uriah, but ultimately, he did by placing him in the front lines of battle.

I sometimes wonder why David was a man after God's own heart. David did some really bad things. Maybe it is to show that no one is perfect and we all have done things of which we aren't proud. But if God calls David a man after His own heart, then why can't I be?

Eventually, David confesses everything to the prophet Nathan. Nathan told David, "The Lord has taken away your sin. You are not going to die. But because by doing this you have made the enemies of the Lord show utter contempt, the son born to you will die."

"David pleaded with God for the child. He fasted and went into his house and spent the nights lying on the ground. The elders of his household stood beside him to get him up from the ground, but he refused, and he would not eat any food with them."

The child soon died.

When David got news that his son passed away, "He got up from the ground. After he had washed, put on lotions and changed his clothes, he went into the house of the Lord and worshipped. Then he went to his house, and at his request they served him food, and he ate."

This story used to baffle me. It may baffle you. So, David's son died, and he is worshipping God. I used to think, is he crazy? What rational person would do this? If one of my friends lost a child and they went to church and started worshipping, I think I would wonder what is wrong with them! I may think that they are drunk, or that grief has robbed them of sanity.

Why is it that when people turn to God in difficult situations, the first inclination most people have is that they're crazy, or they've been brainwashed – drinking too much Kool-Aid at VBS is the common joke people make.

Why is having faith that God has full control over every aspect of life not believable when bad things happen?

Maybe it's easier to think that God is the calmer of storms and not the creator of them? Yet, many people curse God more often in times of trouble than turn to Him for peace and comfort. During these hard times in life we tend to blame God for our storms.

But how many storms arise from decisions we ourselves made?

Many times we don't like to follow the domino path to find where the first domino fell. We just want to find someone to blame for the destruction and scream at God over the rubble.

You may be going through a horrible season in your life filled with trials, but it is in these trials that we need to worship the Lord the most. David was called a man after God's own heart probably because he trusted and praised God in every situation. We too should praise God in every situation, even when it hurts. An interesting song to worship to is "Even When It Hurts (Praise Song)" by Hillsong United.

———————

It is so easy to praise God when you are standing on a mountain top, above all the chaos and stormy clouds. It shows that you have risen above all that is sad and cold in the world and you have made it through.

How often are you on that mountain?

Looking back, are you on a mountain more than you are crawling through the valley?

When I look back, my days in the valley far outweigh the days on a mountaintop. Or is it that when I am on the mountain, the days just seem to blend together like they are nothing. Don't get me wrong, I love to be on the mountain with God. But usually when I get to the peak, I lose my focus on Him. There is no reason to pray to Him when everything is going smoothly (so I think). There is no reason to sing songs of God's blessings and protection when I feel protected and blessed (so I think). There is no reason to cling to a God who will not let me go when I am planted on solid ground (so I think). I often think wrong.

In my memory, I have had moments when my faith was the strongest. I have had months when I felt God was attached at my hip. I have had weeks when I was in constant dialogue with God, because He was the only one I could truly confide in and in whom I could lose myself. When I look at the struggles surrounding those periods, there wasn't much joy – if any. It was not a time I would like to trek through again. They were messy days, days when life was beating me down, and I had the bruises to show for it. Even though I don't want to, I'd go through it all again if it brought me closer to my God.

Funny isn't it. Our faith gets stronger when we are at our weakest. When we are at our weakest, those are the moments we see God's power more clearly. When we see Him more clearly, that's when we praise Him the most.

If you feel like you are left for dead, it is the time to praise God.

A favorite Psalm of mine is Psalm 27. I love how it starts,

"The Lord is my light and my salvation – whom shall I fear? The Lord is the stronghold of my life – of whom shall I be afraid?" Psalm 27:1 New International Version

Why should I be afraid when life happens? Why should I run for cover when I get bad news? Is God not still God? Did He take a day off and lose all His sovereignty? No. God is still my light and my salvation. He is still going to be the rock I cling to.

"One thing I ask of the Lord, this is what I seek: that I may dwell in the house of the Lord all the days of my life, to gaze upon the beauty of the Lord and to seek Him in His temple. For in the day of trouble He will keep me safe in His dwelling; He will hide me in the shelter of His tabernacle and set me high upon a rock. Then my head will be exalted above the enemies who surround me; at His tabernacle will I sacrifice

with shouts of joy; I will sing and make music to the Lord."
Psalm 27:4-6 New International Version

When I was going through high school and college I would get to church hours before the service started. I would sneak back into a hidden room and find a piano and just play and sing to God. I couldn't play or sing very well, but it was my time with God. Teenage years are rough, mine were not that smooth. But whenever I felt sad I could come to a piano and find God through the ivories. "That I may dwell in the house of the Lord all the days of my life." What better place is there to be than in the house of the Lord? Every once in a while I would hear someone coming down the hall, and I would stop playing and hide. I didn't want people to find me. I didn't want people to find my spot where I communed with God. It was my secret place. As I sit back and write, I can recall that tiny room to the smallest detail. The old, painted, black, upright piano, with a pink seat cushion, and an old print of Jesus hanging directly over a vase of plastic flowers that sat on the piano. It was as if God was watching me play for Him. I am feeling peace, just thinking about that room.

I hope you all have a place where you can go. The house of the Lord doesn't have to be a church. It can be a sanctuary in your bedroom, a closet, your backyard. Just please, find your secret place and meet God there often.

Where is yours?

A song that I love to sing when everything is going great is, "Blessed Be Your Name" by Matt Redman. A song that I love to sing when everything is going terribly wrong is, "Blessed Be Your Name." We need to bless God's holy name in every situation. When life is floating by on a peaceful stream, praise Him. When life is crashing about like a hurricane, praise Him. There should not be a reason that we don't praise the Lord of everything. There is no excuse. We need to praise Him.

The book of Job is a good example of how, one minute we're on the mountaintop, and the next, we're wandering through the desert. Job was a very wealthy man with a large family. Instantly, everything was taken away from him except for his wife and some "friends." Job struggled for some time while his friends and his wife were telling him to curse God and die. Quit holding onto a faith in a God who would do this to you. Just curse him and die. Job did not curse God. Job may have questioned why some things were happening, but Job never questioned God's glory. Job was eventually restored to a life better than what he had. He was given more children, more land, more servants – God blessed him.

"The Lord gave and the Lord has taken away; may the name of the Lord be praise. " Job 1:21b New International Version

I highly recommend finding "Blessed Be Your Name" on the internet, Youtube, Spotify, Pandora, whatever means you have and play it. Sing it. Shout it. Give God praise. You may be in your desert, but God still deserves your praises.

May this song open your eyes and your heart to praise God. Blessed is God's glorious name.

———————

Another favorite song of mine is called, "Desert Song." It was written by Brooke Fraser, a worship leader with Hillsong. I don't know how someone can hear this song and not feel the ups and downs of a faith-filled life. Each line encompasses so much depression, yet so much optimism. Go online and have a worship time with just you and God with this song. Let the words transform you.

Even though there is much pain, there is also much hope. I don't know what you are going through right now, but what I do know is that God is still God. Run into His arms. Feel the hope. Drink of His never ceasing water of refreshment. Enter His presence with dirty hands and feet, and bathe in His grace.

———————

May you always worship God, even when the days are long, the nights are lonely, the plate is empty, and the cup is dry.

Worship Him in all circumstances.

Chapter 10

Restoration
Every Morning Is New

We all need restoring every once in a while. It may just be a few touchups here and there, or we may need a full faith makeover. The restoration process is not easy. But if you proceed, it feels so good when you're finished.

One lady that we all know and love had a huge restoration in the early 1980s. In her lifetime, she endured the salty, sea air, the wear and tear of storms, and other deteriorations that come with age. The lady is Lady Liberty.

In the late nineteenth century, the people of France wanted to show their gratitude to the United States for their friendship. The Statue of Liberty was sculpted by Frederic Auguste Bartholdi to be completed in the year 1876, the centennial of the American Declaration of Independence.

In May of 1982, President Ronald Reagan, started to restore the symbol of freedom. They raised funds to tackle the extensive project, and after most of the money was received the restoration process began. It took two years for the work to be completed. But the Statue of Liberty was finished before its centennial celebration on July 4, 1986.

Including the general repairs to the outside of the statue, they made many improvements such as replacing the torch, replacing the iron bands that hold the statue's copper skin to its frame and the installation of an elevator.

The statue was probably as beautiful or more beautiful than it had ever been. But it took two years to complete this massive job. Restoration takes time, but it is definitely worth the wait.

————————

Have you ever experienced an improvement or a restoration of a home? When I was in middle school I survived the destruction of our old bathroom and the construction of a new one. It was an interesting period, because we only had one bathroom and there were four of us living under the same roof at this time. A few days without a bathroom, well, it was an adventure.

It was fascinating to see all the old be tossed aside – the tan tiles, the wooden cabinets, the drywall, everything was gone. All that remained were the wooden beams holding everything intact. It was a little startling how everything can be demolished in a matter of hours, but rebuilding takes days.

Isn't that like life? We can work so hard on a project at work or our reputation, but one wrong move, one bad decision, and it can all be destroyed.

Do you like it when something of yours gets destroyed? No. Who enjoys watching one of their possessions get broken, stained, or ripped? No one. So it is reasonable that when our life crumbles, we don't appreciate it.

Sometimes it's like we are standing in the ruins of our life. We pick up the fragments of what used to be, and now there are just bits and boards. It is hard to have a faithful perspective of something beautiful when everything falls apart.

About 20 years ago, I was having a Bible study. We were discussing the parable of the two builders,

"Anyone who listens to My teaching and follows it is wise, like a person who builds a house on solid rock. Though the rain comes in torrents and the floodwaters rise and wind beat against the house, it won't collapse because it is built on a bedrock. But anyone who hears My teaching and doesn't obey it is foolish, like a person who builds a house on sand. When the rains and floods come and the winds beat against that house, it will collapse with a mighty crash." Matthew 7:24-27 New Living Translation

We were discussing the parable about getting our life straight with God and focusing on our firm foundation when someone put forth a startling notion. "There have been times when I built my dream home, and it was perfect. Sometimes the scariest seasons in life, are the seasons of contentment. Content with my relationship with God, then slowly, my dream home starts to crumble. It isn't that God is mad, but God always has something better. To embrace the best of God is sometimes to let go and let Him destroy what you call good."

I sat hypnotized by the honesty in her words. I also sat in awe of the faith she emitted. Because her life was a proof of her devotion to God. I had not ever realized before that day that sometimes when God destroys us, it is to build us up bigger and better than before.

———————

There is a motto that I say to my friends all the time that God is both a builder and a wrecking ball. To be honest, I don't like the fact that God is swinging a giant metal ball to demolish my life. When I see a wrecking ball it swings like a pendulum, at a great force and wreaks havoc on anything that comes its way. It also seems so big that it can't be precise. Does the wrecking ball have good aim? When I see it hit buildings, I wonder if the operator meant to hit that exact brick or does it really matter because the whole building is coming down?

The difference between a careless wrecking ball and God is God is in control.

That may be the only comfort I find when I feel the cement crack beneath my toes. But that should not be the only comfort. The Bible is filled with God's promises to lift up His children, to protect His children, to love His children. But how does destroying show love? His love is shown by restoring us better than before.

Are you ready to be demolished to be built back up better than ever? Do you trust Him to be the Builder?

———————

Lament means to feel or express sorrow, remorse, or regret. The book of Lamentations is just that, a book of sorrow. The book was written by the weeping prophet, Jeremiah, who we discussed earlier in the book. It is a book of sadness, but in the middle of the short book is a chapter of hope – one of my favorite verses.

"Yet this I call to mind and therefore I have hope: Because of the Lord's great love we are not consumed, for His compassions never fail. They are new every morning; great is Your faithfulness. I say to myself, 'The Lord is my portion; therefore I will wait for Him.' The Lord is good to those who hope in Him, to the one who seeks Him; it is good to wait quietly for the salvation of the Lord." Lamentations 3:21-26 New International Version

God's mercies are new every morning. When you are about to fall asleep, rehashing the days regrettable moments, know that

God's mercies are new every day. Pray for help to have a better tomorrow. When you feel like you are never going to get through the week, and it is just Tuesday, God's mercies are new every day. Pray for help to get through the week. God is there to help you. Look to the solver of all problems to be the solution.

I mentioned in Chapter 2 about hope and our need for it. Here we see again the importance of hope. "The Lord is good to those who hope in Him." Don't lose your hope. Don't lose heart.

I love that phrase, don't lose heart. It's the start of a great chapter on perseverance, 2 Corinthians 4.

"Therefore, we do not lose heart. Though outwardly we are wasting away, yet inwardly we are being renewed day by day. For our light and momentary troubles are achieving for us an eternal glory that far outweighs them all. So we fix our eyes not on what is seen, but on what is unseen. For what is seen is temporary, but what is unseen is eternal." 2 Corinthians 4:16-18 New International Version

The word renew is very similar to restore. It is taking away all that is weighing you down and bringing you back to your best. Who wants to be renewed to an okay life? Who wants to be restored to a plain life? No, He wants to restore you to your best.

But have you ever been at your best?

Probably not...we can always get better. So, when you are going to be restored or renewed, you may not be the same person you were...you may be better.

A cool example of renewing you to a better life is the life of a caterpillar. It goes about its day crawling on the ground, eating leaves that it can reach, seeing only what its neck allows it to see. A caterpillar's life may be boring because they are fairly slow, and they have to crawl everywhere. That is until a miraculous transformation, and it is miraculous. How does every caterpillar know to get inside a cocoon and after some time in a shell emerge with wings? God is a genius. Nature is so cool, and His glory is shown in every aspect of it. The butterfly is now able to fly quicker than a caterpillar used to crawl. It can see more from being in the air. It has more possibilities.

Given a choice, would you stay as a caterpillar or embark on the journey to become a butterfly?

In our faith process, we all want an easy growth, but many times in order to grow you have to leave some things behind. You can't hold onto old ways, old friends, old situations or old habits if a change is going to occur. It would be so easy for the caterpillar to get ready to get into cocoon and then think, nope, not going. It's dark in there. And I have to leave my family and friends. And whose to say something is going to happen? I'm fine being bird food.

So many people stop during this process of restoration because it is painful. The first thing that has be torn down is pride. The notion that you thought your way was good, but it really wasn't is a hard realization.

If you can't surrender to humility, you will never be restored.

Are you ready to surrender?

In Chapter 4, I spoke of blind faith, and the need to step out in faith.

"So we fix our eyes not on what is seen, but on what is unseen."

We need to keep believing with faith in what we cannot see. We need to hold firm in what we can't fully understand. God is so big, and He sees all. We don't need to see to believe it; we just need to trust that God sees it. That should be assurance enough for us.

Sometimes you have to take a scary step inside your "cocoon" to emerge as something better. Don't be afraid. God won't let you down. He never has. He never will.

Do you trust Him to be faithful?

If you had the opportunity to buy regular washing detergent or buy the new and improved washing detergent – both cost the same – which one would you buy? If it was me, the new and improved. We all like new things. When Apple comes out with their new version of iPhone, people don't usually say, "Well, I have the old one, so I am good." No, if they have the money they will go and buy the new version.

For people who love fashion, if someone said they would buy you a new outfit, would you get the latest threads or a dead fad from the 70's? Most would buy the new, except for some who may have some eclectic taste. New usually means better. You don't want to drink old milk because you might get sick, and you don't want to eat stale bread because who wants to eat a hard BP&J?

A verse that is perfect for trading the old for the new is:

"Therefore, if anyone is in Christ, he is a new creation; the old has gone, the new has come." 2 Corinthians 5:17 New International Version

God doesn't want us to be old (not meaning age). He wants us to be new. He wants us to be fresh. He wants us to be filled with life. He wants us to enjoy the new today and not dread the old past. He wants us to be ready for what is in store after we have been restored.

I pray that you see the beauty in restoration.

I hope that you cling to God during the process of renewal.

The first renewal is the hardest, because it is unfamiliar, but step inside the cocoon of uneasiness and rest in the arms of peace. You are going to be better than ever.

The new and improved you.

Chapter 11

What Is Yours?
Stories of Faith

As you can tell in this book, I have many favorite verses and chapters in the Bible. How can you not have many favorites since all of it is God's Word? I guess all of it should be my favorite, but there are some that stand out above the rest.

One chapter, the chapter that brought out the purpose of this book is Hebrews 11 – The Hall of Faith. Please go and read this chapter and stand amazed at those listed.

When I read this chapter I can't help but see all the individuals with their great faith and realize that these are ordinary people. Did they realize that hundreds of years after their faithful service to God that they would be listed as some of the great people of faith? I sometimes wonder if this chapter was written after I was alive, would my name be listed here?

Would your name?

We all have stories, and no one person's story is better than another's. Because when we each take a step of faith, heaven is rejoicing. Heaven does not care the size of the step, but only that a step forward was taken.

I purposely waited to write this chapter until Chapter 11. I wanted this chapter to be "Our Hall of Faith." This may be strange, but I want you to share your stories of faith so we all can read them. Don't be shy. Tell your stories proudly, because you are not bringing glory to yourself, but to God who performed these incredible feats. Recall those times in your life where you took a step of faith, and God honored it. It's great to read the stories of faith that happened thousands of years ago, but when we see God moving today, I get even more excited. Just as it is stated in Hebrews 13:8,

"Jesus Christ is the same yesterday and today and forever." New International Version

If God performed miracles in the past, He can definitely perform them today. When we take a step of faith tomorrow, why should we doubt when we know that God is still the same?

I think this is a perfect way to encourage one another by proclaiming miracles, so when there is a day that your faith is low and you need assurance of God's faithfulness, we can cling to one another's stories. God is faithful.

———————

When I am alone in my car, Sara Groves' song, *When the Saints* is one I sing at the top of my lungs. Its message is one we all should strive to imitate. She sings about various people throughout history and the mark they made with their faith.

116

I hope that when we all get to Heaven, and we see the saints of old marching, I want my life of faith to be shown. I want to be one of them.

I pray that you have a story of faith to share. If you don't, don't be disappointed. Tell us what you are still waiting in faith for. Tell us so we can pray that God gives you strength during this time. Tell us so we can encourage you in your faithful journey. Tell us as a way of proclaiming what God is going to do in the future.

May you get as much joy in telling your stories as I will get from reading them. God is so good, and we need to express His goodness to everyone.

As it says in Romans 12:15,

"Rejoice with those who rejoice, and mourn with those who mourn." New International Version

May these stories of faith cause us to rejoice with the saints and angels and lift up those who need encouraging.

Please go to my website a tell us your story.

https://ericsuddoth.wordpress.com/our-hall-of-faith/

Chapter 12

It's a Process

Every major innovation had a process. There are steps involved, because usually when you come up with an idea, you don't see it put into action the same instant. One example is the Wright Brothers' Invention Process:

Researched How Things Fly (1899 – 1902)

Developed Flight Control Systems (1900 – 1902)

Tested Theories (1901 – 1902)

Developed Test Pilot Skills (1900 – 1905)

Developed Propulsion System (1903 – 1920's)

The First Flight (December 17, 1903)

Flight Development (1904 – 1907)

Pushing the Envelope (1904 – Beyond)

Overview of Wright Brothers' Invention Process

http://wright.nasa.gov/overview.htm

Look at the dates listed beside the steps of the process. Many dates run simultaneously with other steps. They tested theories for two years. During this time they were also researching and developing. Some would think that you would research, then develop, then test. But do we always succeed on our first test? No.

The Wright brothers' tested many different theories, but they didn't stop at their first failed attempt. They persevered until they figured out a way to fly.

We always hear about the Wright brothers' first flight on December 17, 1903, which lasted 12 seconds. We rarely hear about the following events. They continued their work and their research to design better aircrafts. Eventually, they were able to stay in flight for up to half an hour, perform air maneuvers and even take passengers for a ride. (Their process for flight is the same process still used by NASA engineers to solve problems. Just an interesting tidbit.)

If first you don't succeed…don't quit. If the Wright brothers' quit, who knows where we would be?

If you quit on your dream, who knows where the world will be next year?

———————

Yes, faithfully following your dreams is a process. It's like a rollercoaster. You will experience steep inclines and dramatic drops. There will probably be days that will run smooth, and you start to see all the pieces falling into place. Then a curve ball comes and smashes a near finished picture. You can give up on your dreams, or you can pick yourself up and follow God.

I wish I could tell you that acquiring God's dream for your life is going to be easy, but that would be a lie. Read what Christ says to the disciples before His crucifixion.

"Jesus asked, 'Do you finally believe? But the time is coming – indeed it's here now – when you will be scattered, each one going his own way, leaving Me alone. Yet I am not alone because the Father is with Me. I have told you all this so that you may have peace in Me. Here on earth you will have many trials and sorrows. But take heart, because I have overcome the world." John 16:31-33 New Living Translation

We have to read this verse in context because earlier Christ was telling His followers about God's plan, which He told them many times before in parables. This time He flat out told them that He was going to have to leave. Suddenly, they said that they understood what He was saying and believed that Jesus came from God. Jesus tells them that they were going to leave Him when persecution comes, but I think it relates in our journey of faith as well. When you feel like a failure, are tired of trying, tired of hearing snickering behind your back, *take heart, because I have overcome the world."* We cannot handle the world by ourselves, but with Jesus, what else do we need? If God is on our side, who can be against us!

"Do you finally believe?" Jesus asked His friends. I can hear Him recalling all the miracles He performed where His friends were eyewitnesses. He must have been saddened. Because for the last three years, Jesus had spent every waking moment with this small group of men, and they just finally believed.

Look at all the stories in the Bible. Listen to other believers' stories of faith. Look back at your own memory and see how God moved.

Then why do we sometimes not believe?

Can you hear Jesus asking you, "Do you finally believe?"

I know in this book I have repeated myself many times. I just want you to always remember God's faithfulness to you. It is said that the average person has to do something 16 to 21 times before it becomes a habit. I repeat God's faithfulness, not that it becomes a habit, per se, but that you have a habit of remembering it.

When I was in high school, all the seniors had to write down a quote to be printed in our yearbooks. My quote was a verse from Proverbs which I still hold dear:

"Commit to the Lord whatever you do, and your plans will succeed." Proverbs 16:3 New Living Translation

In your process, if you have not fully committed your plan into God's sturdy hands, right now is the best time to just lay it down. When you trust Him and follow Him, how can you go wrong or veer off course?

Are you ready to lay it down?

"Trust in the Lord with all your heart and lean not on your own understanding; in all your ways acknowledge Him and He will make your paths straight." Proverbs 3:5-6 New International Version

When we trust God with everything, and I mean everything, you may feel like you're falling. It is an unsettling feeling to figuratively jump from a ledge. Yet you won't crash, because God will be there to catch you.

I sometimes trust God with all my heart, but I have a hard time not leaning on my intelligence. When God says for us to trust, we need to trust Him – mind, body and soul. We need to trust Him even when it doesn't make sense. When God tells us to do something, we need to follow, no matter how extravagant it may sound. It may be something as simple as speaking to a stranger. Who knows what the stranger is going through? God knows. If He tells you to speak, you need to speak.

The same can be said if He wants you to slow down and be quiet. Sometimes we get so wrapped up in our plans and agendas and getting everything finished, that we sometimes miss God.

Slowing down may be a major step in trusting God, because God's timing is perfect. Rest in His perfect timing. I don't believe there are any coincidences. If we stop listening to God and start doing things our way, everything that we worked so hard for may fall apart. When we take God out of the equation – the God who is holding everything together – who is to say He won't let some of it fall apart to wake us up?

Has He ever woken you up before?

————————

An album that radiates God's love and faithfulness, while wrestling with doubt and confusion, is Audrey Assad's *Evergreen*. My favorite song on the album is at the conclusion, "Drawn to You." It's a gentle reminder that even though life is hard, we are flawed, and even though we are all that and more, God is still God. And that is something remarkable.

I like to imagine a God of love that makes sure that His child lives a good life, sheltered from pain and harm. But God never promises us that shallow, self-centered life. When we follow Him, it may cost everything. But when we follow Him, what we may give up is nothing compared to what we will receive. Not in monetary means, but in a relationship that is solid and deeply rooted in truth. This process may be hard, but during it, I hope you are drawn to Him. Even when the world says to give up, you are crazy, why waste your time? I hope you sense there is something special in following Him. Are you feeling drawn to Him? If not, why?

———

I wish I could tell you that if you believe in faith and hope unswervingly, that you will achieve your plans in three days. But God doesn't work on a timeline or use a calendar. His timing is different than ours. That doesn't mean you should give up. If you feel that God laid a plan/goal on your heart, keep at it. He knows that it may not be easy, that is why He gave us the Holy Spirit to be our Counselor and comfort us.

Do not neglect the Holy Spirit. Go to the Holy Spirit with pure reverence. Ask for comfort when you need it. Ask for guidance when you need counseling. Ask for anything that you need, because He gives generously.

"The Lord will fulfill His purpose for me; your love, O Lord, endures forever – do not abandon the works of Your hands." Psalm 138:8 New International Version

God is faithful and His love for you is eternal. Please, do not give up on your plan. God will fulfill His purpose for you, but God needs you to keep the faith and keep going. God can do everything, but He wants you to work through. Every time I think that, I can't help but feel motivated. God chose me to write this book, just like He chose you to do something. Please, do not abandon the works of your hands.

Look back at some of the stories that I mentioned before. If Christopher Columbus never took a step of faith, if Dr. Jenner never believed there was something more, if Colonel Sanders didn't persevere, who knows where we would be?

If you give up, who will finish it?

————————

"I have fought the good fight, I have finished the race, I have kept the faith." 2 Timothy 4:7 New International Version

Having faith is like a fight. If you think faith is easy, tell me the secret. True faith is hard. You have to stand firm to the punches the world throws. You have to bob and weave from insults, doubts, and the crushing blow of self-inflicted pessimism. If you are not prepared, you will be knocked out in the first round.

This is where daily prayer and scripture reading are essential. Talk to God. Read His words. Listen to God. Meditate on His Word. Start listening to Christian music. I'm not saying anything negative against secular music. But if you want to be lifted up, listen to Christian music. Whatever genre you enjoy, there is music.

Have your own personal worship service. Give God the glory in your own special way. That means more to Him than going through the motions, which He despises. Be real.

When you have finished your race, rejoice. Tell the world what God has done. Shout it from the rooftops. Don't be ashamed at what God has done for you. Sometimes we fear becoming self-obsessed so we never tell others what we are doing. When you put God in the stage light, it is all for His glory. Tell, tell, tell.

When you have achieved your dream remember that the first step was faith. You can't gain your full potential when you lose faith. When you lose faith in what God calls you to do, you actually lose faith in God. Don't even doubt what you can do, because you can do all things through Christ. You can do everything.

Fight. Finish. Keep the faith.

———————

When you have fulfilled your dream, tell, tell, tell!

"But in your hearts set apart Christ as Lord. Always be prepared to give an answer to everyone who asks you to give the reason for the hope that you have. But do this with gentleness and respect." 1 Peter 3:15 New International Version

When you tell what you accomplished, this may be an opening to share your faith. Could the reason God gave you your dream, ultimately, so that you could share the love of Christ? The purpose we are on earth is to share the Gospel so all may come and know Christ. God is so wise. What if at the end of every dream, is the telling of the Good News, which is the love of Christ.

God has a purpose for every man. No believer is void of a purpose. The main purpose we have is to share our faith. What if God combines our personal purpose with every man's purpose? What if the sharing of Christ is really our mission laced with a flowery exterior of our dream.

May you achieve your dream that God planted in you, so you can cause someone else to start dreaming a dream that God planted in them.

It's time to be a trend setter.

Are you ready to change the world?

You could be the one God uses. Who knows how far your little dream will reach?

Chapter 13

To Be ~~Continued~~ Continuing

One of my favorite television series was the spy show *Alias* starring Jennifer Garner as Sydney Bristow, the ultimate spy. Every episode had a cliffhanger. I always hated it when someone on the show was in a difficult situation, and they couldn't solve the issue in the last two minutes. The audience had to wait for a week to know what happened. It was so nerve-racking. I knew that they usually never killed off their main stars, but with each episode, I was glued to the screen wondering how Sydney Bristow was going to get herself out of the situation.

Life is not like a television show, thank God. Sometimes it is as complex as an *Alias* episode with double agents and roundhouse kicks. Then other days, it is like *Seinfeld* in their crazy antics of no reasoning. Thankfully, God never ends us with a To Be Continued. No, our life is continuing.

You may believe that since your dream has been fulfilled you can sit back, relax and enjoy the rest of your life. You pat yourself on the back and bask in the fact that God's plan for your life has been accomplished.

Do you really believe that?

Do you believe that God only has one dream for your life?

Let's look again at a key verse

"'For I know the plans I have for you,' declares the Lord, 'plans to prosper you and not to harm you, to give you hope and a future.'" Jeremiah 29:11 New International Version

Do you see that the word plan is plural? God has plans for your life. He has many, many dreams. Most of the time, our brains cannot expand our minds beyond what we believe all there is. Look at scientists. Many years ago, they believed that the earth was the only thing out there. Later, they realized there were other planets which formed our Solar System. Most believed that this was all there was. Now we find out that there are billions of galaxies, and our Solar System is just a dot in the Milky Way Galaxy.

The same can be said with cells. Scientists believed that a cell was the smallest thing. That was until they broke one up and found all the gunk that we learn about in biology class.

Do you really believe that all that you have dreamed is all that God dreams for your life?

If you do, it is time to get a "telescope or microscope" on your life. There is so much more.

———

If you are truly honest with yourself, you may wish that God only gave you one dream in your life. Look back at how long you have had your current dream, and see how long it took or is taking for your dream to reach its fulfillment.

It was probably a long, hard journey and now I am telling you that you have to start from scratch and begin the journey all over.

Well, maybe, but maybe not.

Whatever your dream may be, it could be small, and God may want to expand on it. He may want to get more people involved who have similar interests and radically change your neighborhood, city, nation, or even the world. We should never underestimate God, because since He gave you the itch that needed scratching, He might have wanted it to spread like poison ivy.

If you look at your dream like a game of chess, you may have thought that achieving your hope was a checkmate. In God's viewpoint, it may have been just the very first move in a great game.

Are you going to be brave enough to move another pawn?

On the other side, your dream may have reached its potential, and God may have something totally different on the horizon. Are you anxious to take a peak at the rising dream? Or are you scared at what you may see.

If you are scared, just remember what you have already gone through. Look back at your miracle and see how God moved.

When God calls you to move again, and He will, remember that He is faithful. He is God, and He will never let you be alone. He may let you go to test your faith, but He is always nearby.

Watching a young bird learn to fly is a frightening experience. The mother bird pushes the baby bird from the nest in hopes that he/she starts flapping its wings before it hits the ground. The same can be said with how my grandfather taught us all to swim. When we were kids, he would take us in a boat and just throw us out. He was always there in case we needed him. But we usually kicked our legs and swung our arms to stay afloat.

It's sometimes hard to be thrown into a lake of water, but it is in those instances that we learn the most. We either sink or swim.

Are you ready to swim again?

———

This chapter is hard for me to write, because I have no clue what God has in store for my next dream. I love to dream and come up with ideas, and I have plenty of them. Finding my passion, the one that God will give life to, well, I'm a little apprehensive about that myself.

May we all find that God is a God of endless possibilities. That He is the God who performed miracles in the past, and He is the God who will perform miracles still. Let's walk this narrow road of faith wherever God directs. May we have hope in the darkest nights that God will raise the sun for another morning where His mercies are always new. May we be certain that God will not lead us astray and that our goals are attainable with Jesus Christ. Lastly, may we wander blindly into the exterior of the unknown with assurance that God is holding our hand.

When life gets hard, remember that trials come so we can mature. Would you rather be a dirty rock of gold, caked in soil, or a refined necklace on display for all to see and admire. May your faith become of greater worth than gold.

Remember to pray. I hope you don't have to remember to pray, but constantly pray. God wants to hear from you, but He also wants you to hear from Him. Prayer is a conversation, so converse with God. Maybe take Him out on date.

And lastly, praise Him. Praise Him for who He is and what He is doing. Because He is doing something even when you cannot see it. He is working on your dream, lining up pieces for when the time is right. Just praise the God of the universe, the King of Heaven and of Earth. Give Him worship that would please Him.

May we hold firm to the promises of God's love and always remember

"Now faith is being sure of what we hope for and certain of what we do not see." Hebrews 11:1 New International Version

God bless you in your journey of faith, and may you embrace the ever faithful God. And this is not the end, it is just a continuation.

References

The Holy Bible, New International Version (NIV) © 1973,1978, 1984, 2011 by Biblica, Inc.

The Holy Bible, New King James Version (NKJV) © 1984 by Thomas Nelson, Inc.

The Holy Bible, New Living Translation © 2004 by Tyndale House Publishers.

The Holy Bible, The Message © 2005 by NavPress.

The Holy Bible, English Standard Version (ESV) © 2007 by Crossway Bibles.

The Holy Bible, International Standard Version (ISV) © 2011 by The ISV Foundation.

The Holy Bible, The Bible in Basic English (BBE) © 1965 by Cambridge University Press.

The Holy Bible, New International Reader's Version (NIRV) © 1995, 1996, 1998, 2014 by Biblica, Inc.

Chapter 1

Chris Rice. "Eighth Grade." *Run the Earth, Watch the Sky.* Rocketown Records. 2003.

Chapter 2

Sara Groves. "Jeremiah." *The Other Side of Something.* INO Records. 2004.

Talbot, John Michael. *The Lessons of St. Francis: How to Bring Simplicity and Spirituality into Your Daily Life.* Plume. 1998. Print.

Chapter 4

Ginny Owens and Kyle Matthews. "If You Want Me To." *Without Condition.* Rocketown Records. 1999.

Ginny Owens. Traditional Irish Hymn. "Be Thou My Vision." *Without Condition.* Rocketown Records. 1999.

Chapter 5

Chris Tomlin and Reuben Morgan. "Awakening." *Passion: Awakening.* sixstepsrecords. 2010.

Chapter 7

Nichole Nordeman. "Small Enough." *This Mystery.* Sparrow Records. 2000.

Chapter 8

Sara Groves. *The Other Side of Something*. INO Records. 2004.

Steven Furtick, Matt Redman, Chris Brown and Mack Brock. "Do It Again." *There is a Cloud*. Elevation Church, Provident Label Group. 2017.

Chapter 9

Joel Houston. "Even When It Hurts (Praise Song)." *Empires*. Hillsong, Sparrow, Capital CMG. 2015.

Matt Redman and Beth Redman. "Blessed Be Your Name." *Where Angels Fear to Tread*. Survivor. 2002.

Brooke Fraser. "Desert Song." *This is Our God*. Hillsong. 2008.

Chapter 11

Sara Groves. "When the Saints." *Tell Me What You Know*. INO Records. 2007.

Chapter 12

"Re-Living The Wright Way." *National Aeronautics and Space Administration, NASA*, http://wright.nasa.gov/overview.htm

Audrey Assad. "Drawn to You." *Evergreen*. Fortunate Fall Records. 2018.

Connect with Eric Suddoth

Website   https://ericsuddoth.wordpress.com/
Facebook @eric.suddoth.author
Twitter @EricSuddoth
Instagram ericsuddoth

If interested in having Eric Suddoth speak at your church, small group gatherings or conferences, please contact him through his website.

www.ingramcontent.com/pod-product-compliance
Lightning Source LLC
Chambersburg PA
CBHW021128020426
42331CB00005B/668